TruStory

Beyond the Pain

This is a work of memoir. The events and experiences described in this book are true to the best of the author's recollection. Some names and identifying details have been changed to protect the privacy of certain individuals.

ISBN:9798270311254

Published in the United States of America

First Edition: 2025

Cover Photo: Atala Photography
(RAWShttps://hopp.bio/atalaphotography)

Instagram: @atala_photography; Facebook: Atala Photography

Book design and layout by Amazon Kindle Direct Publishing

Printed in the United States

Proof/Editing: Ishevetta Campanale

Dedication

To my mother (Rachel D. Patterson-Ford),

A woman whose love for her family always shined brighter than her adversities.

Preface

This writing reflects a powerful journey of self-discovery and resilience. It conveys a deep sense of liberation from fear and burdens that have weighed down the soul. The author views her past struggles not as mistakes, but as essential parts of her life's design, shaping her understanding of purpose and growth.

The emotions expressed are raw and sincere, revealing moments of vulnerability where fear once influenced decisions. Yet, through reflection and a renewed commitment to personal growth, the author emerges stronger, embracing gratitude and openness. The determination to break free from unhealthy patterns creates a compelling narrative of healing aimed at laying a foundation not only for oneself but also for future generations.

There is a beautiful warmth in the desire to uplift others, emphasizing the importance of community and connection in healing. The author expresses a sincere wish to support those who struggle, recognizing that everyone has their own battles and that sometimes, shared strength is essential to overcoming hardship. The phrase "Beyond the Pain" is a rallying cry that emphasizes a bold commitment to truth and authenticity.

The reflections on happiness, joy, and peace challenge conventional views, focusing instead on the depth of love, the timelessness of passion, and the calm found in self-acceptance.

Ultimately, this writing highlights the journey of healing, not as a destination, but as an ongoing process filled with light, hope, and the unwavering belief that with effort and heart, a brighter path can be created.

Introduction

I truly believe that sharing our personal stories can inspire others. Our unique experiences can serve as vital lifelines for those feeling isolated in their struggles, offering a sense of connection and understanding. This journey of introspection has led me to explore and reflect deeply on core aspects of life, including spirituality, authenticity, love, friendship, marriage, parenting, purpose, confidence, and self-worth. These elements are key to creating a fulfilled and happy life.

In my pursuit of genuine happiness, I have read insightful books, engaged in meaningful conversations, and explored various ways of self-exploration. Each effort has been driven by one central question: "How can I find true happiness?" This question has helped me uncover essential truths about myself and the world around me, guiding me toward a deeper understanding of how to live a fulfilling life.

On July 26, 2023, I reached a breaking point, feeling overwhelmed and defeated by my emotions. During this difficult moment, I chose to share an honest and heartfelt post on social media, exposing my struggles for all to see. Despite doing extensive research on grief, depression symptoms, and anxiety management, I felt I was missing a crucial piece of my emotional puzzle. This missing link could unlock a deeper understanding of my situation and lead to healing.

As I read more books and articles, life kept throwing challenges my way and I questioned whether true happiness would ever possible. It was hard to see joy amid the daily demands of motherhood, balancing time and finances, navigating changing family and friendship dynamics, planning my wedding with excitement—and stress—the difficult process of blending families, my pursuit of personal growth, and dealing with serious health concerns that loomed like a dark cloud. Despite this overwhelming list of challenges and persistent doubts, I chose to trust in God. I decided to stay committed to sharing my truth, embracing vulnerability as a source of strength rather than weakness.

In these pages, I hope to honestly share my journey, highlighting both the euphoric highs and painful lows I experienced. I aim to share lessons I've learned and practical tools that helped me manage painful emotions and move closer to finding—and maintaining—my true happiness. Through my story, I want to inspire others in similar situations, reminding them that they are not alone and that joy can be regained, even in chaos.

Table of Contents

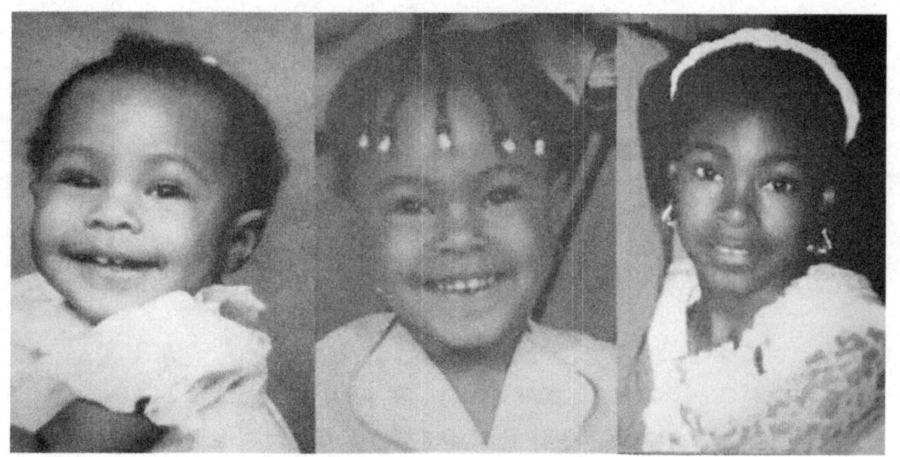

The Young Truchel Lillian Ford

Part One: P.A.I.N.

"Pain grows when you don't grow from the pain."

- C.C. Aurel

Chapter 1
Crippled Inside

The term "crippled inside," as defined by the Cambridge Dictionary, refers to being deeply affected or limited by emotional or psychological challenges. For me, this often manifested as an overwhelming sensitivity to the feelings and emotions of those I loved most. It wasn't until I began unraveling the threads of my past that I recognized how my incessant desire to please others had, I believe, been unintentionally embedded into the fabric of my childhood.

From a young age, I developed a pattern of prioritizing my family and friends' needs over my own. This tendency stemmed from a deep-seated fear of disappointing those I cared about. I believed that I had to sacrifice myself in some way to prove my love. And I worried that if I didn't that, they would misconstrue my self-preservation and care as a lack of love or concern for them if I didn't prioritize them. As a result, I often sacrificed my happiness and well-being in a desperate attempt to ensure that others felt secure and fulfilled.

As I transitioned into young adulthood, I discovered that I could only go so long before I could no longer maintain the façade of my own well-being. Hiding behind a mask of social conventions and polite behavior worked for a while, but eventually, the weight of my suppressed emotions would eventually became unbearable.

Society suggests that, even when bombarded with life's struggles, we should always maintain a positive outlook; easier said than done. In my quest to shield my family from discomfort, I routinely overlooked my emotional struggles. Leaning on phrases like "Be grateful; others have it worse," or "Just move on; you can't change the past," echoed around me and within me, fostering a toxic positivity that discouraged genuine emotional expression.

These societal messages can create the illusion that admitting our feelings is a sign of weakness, leading us to believe that if we openly acknowledge our struggles, we somehow become less capable than those who seem to navigate life's challenges without a hint of self-reflection. It is undoubtedly rewarding to savor the joyous moments in life when everything aligns perfectly. However, the harsh truth is that authentic growth often emerges from our most profound struggles and setbacks. By taking the time to confront and process our emotions, we unlock the door to personal development, allowing virtues such as love, compassion, and empathy to flourish within us.

People given everything on a silver platter often perceive life, love, and success through a lens vastly different from those who have fought valiantly for what they hold dear. Our life experiences shape our perspectives, making it imperative to recognize and honor our feelings rather than suppress them. Acknowledging our emotional landscape isn't merely acceptable but essential for true healing and growth.

I'll admit that coming to this profound realization and embarking on the journey toward true healing and personal growth felt impossible and undeniably terrifying. The thought of allowing my past traumas to resurface to confront my present challenges felt like I was stepping into a living nightmare. Each recollection was not just emotionally overwhelming, but physically sickening, as if I were carrying a heavy weight on my chest that made it hard to breathe.

All the issues I had tried to ignore were clamoring for attention, demanding to be attended to simultaneously, which only intensified my anxiety. The fear of change loomed over me like a dark cloud, filled with unresolved conflicts from my past that threatened to consume me, faced with self-doubt that whispered insidious messages of inadequacy, drowning out any flicker of self-belief. Negative self-talk echoed in my mind, reinforcing my insecurities and amplifying feelings of unworthiness.

Additionally, the outside pressures from friends, family, and society only added to my internal struggle, making me feel like I was under an unrelenting microscope. My natural tendency to avoid discomfort and steer clear of confrontation only complicated matters further. I was caught in a whirlwind of emotions, desperately trying to hold on to my sense of self while feeling like I was on the brink of losing it all.

I deliberately chose to confront each of my challenges with courage and determination, including navigating the complexities of various medical issues that demanded my attention and resilience, and embracing the joyful yet often overwhelming journey of motherhood. The path hasn't always been smooth; it's been punctuated by the dynamics of blending a family, raising concerns over loyalty, and co-parenting disagreements, which frequently tested my strength and resolve.

Through these hurdles, I committed myself to an enriching journey of self-discovery and healing. I delved deep into my emotional landscape, confronting my fears and insecurities head-on. Each step of this process was essential, driven by a desire to emerge as the person God has always envisioned me to be—someone stronger, more empathetic, and truly authentic in every aspect of life.

This commitment to personal growth has become a cornerstone of my existence, guiding me through the complexities of raising children, fostering meaningful relationships, and maintaining a sense of balance within the chaos. As you move forward, I want to share that this is my truth and my journey. I must recognize that nothing about who I am stems solely from my efforts. I am deeply grateful to God for everything I have and for the guidance I've received along the way.

Chapter 2
History of Trauma

Life often becomes complicated, not instantly but gradually through the accumulation of experiences and challenges. These complications don't strike us all at once; instead, they seep into our daily existence like shadows at dusk, adding layers of complexity with each passing day. Small decisions turn into larger dilemmas, and seemingly insignificant events begin to intertwine, forming a web of responsibility, expectation, and emotional weight. As we navigate through these subtle shifts, we may find ourselves at a crossroads, where the simplicity we once took for granted gives way to a more nuanced reality.

Failing to acknowledge and address my feelings and emotions initially simplified my life; however, over time, neglecting these emotions significantly affected multiple aspects of my daily life. Unprocessed emotions hindered my communication and my ability to authentically connect with others, leading to misunderstandings and strained relationships. Moreover, this emotional avoidance eroded my self-worth, as I struggled to recognize and validate my own needs and experiences. Over time, this pattern contributed to heightened stress, anxiety, and difficulty in managing interpersonal dynamics, ultimately diminishing my overall well-being and happiness.

The loss of my mother served as the catalyst that compelled me to confront my past traumas directly. Her absence created a void that forced me to reflect on unresolved pain and experiences that I had long buried. In the year following my mother's passing, I found myself consumed by the weight of my grief, fixated solely on the profound loss I had endured.

It was as if I were standing in a shadow cast by her absence, blind to the strength she'd devoted forty-two years to cultivating within me. I overlooked the unwavering confidence she had always shown in my abilities, the joyous cheers that once echoed through our home, celebrating my victories, no matter how small, and the reassuring safety that only a mother can provide.

I recognize this reflection may come off as selfish. Yet it underscores a critical truth: no matter the perceptions of those around you, including even those of a parent or parents, the most profound and lasting perspective is the one you hold of yourself. I had lost the one person who believed in me more deeply and unconditionally than I ever believed in myself: my mother. Her passing felt like a heavy, irrevocable weight on my heart, yet I understood that God had called her home for a well-deserved rest. She had endured so much throughout her life, and now she could finally embrace tranquility and peace.

At just twenty-four years old, I lost a child while giving birth. My daughter (Madison Jovan Ford) maintained a strong heartbeat all the way up to the time the fluorescent light in the hospital room met the crown of her head. It was a jolting, life-altering experience that left me feeling shattered, vulnerable, and isolated. In the midst of this unimaginable grief, there I was once again finding the strength to push through and navigate the world around me that didn't seem to understand my pain.

There were people around me offering unwanted advice and harsh criticisms, adding to my emotional turmoil. People would say things like, "It's God's plan," or "You can always try again," which, in that moment of grief, felt dismissive and hurtful. Some people even blamed me for the loss, which left me wrestling with guilt and anger.

The reality of me walking into the hospital almost six months pregnant and then leaving the hospital empty-handed made me weak as if my entire world was falling apart. So, I internalized those hurtful comments and the pain of losing my daughter, and I never sought any counseling or outside support. I didn't even know how to find the help I needed, and unfortunately, no one gave me any insight into how to get it. Just as I had much later down the line, when I lost my mother, I played the role of being strong, by putting on a brave face, and trying to hold it together so that I didn't come off as weak or attention-seeking.

In the wake of losing my mother, I realized it was essential for me to become my own source of strength. It was high time I leaned into my capabilities and aspirations, embarking on a journey to grow and unlock my full potential. I acknowledged that I needed to cultivate a belief in myself, to reassure my spirit that

God's purpose for my life would ultimately triumph over the fears that had long held me back. Which meant confronting the detrimental habits that my past had shaped. I learned that my traumas did not have to define me; instead, I could repurpose them into powerful tools for healing and growth. By transforming my pain into lessons of resilience, I aimed to elevate myself and offer support and guidance to others who might be struggling. I sought to turn my challenges into stepping stones, fostering an environment where I could thrive and help others find their strength.

As a child, I often found myself on the receiving end of comments that highlighted my sensitivity and emotional nature, words that would linger in my mind and weigh heavily on my heart. These remarks, often intended as light-hearted observations, left me feeling overlooked and isolated, like an outsider peering in on a world that seemed to operate with a different set of emotional rules. The incessant refrain that I was "too sensitive" reinforced the belief that my feelings were inconsequential and that no one genuinely cared to delve into my perspective or understand the depths of my emotions.

As the years passed, I adapted to this harsh reality by constructing emotional barriers, unknowingly training myself to suppress my feelings and endure discomfort in silence. This coping mechanism, born out of a desire to avoid vulnerability, inadvertently led me to develop a heightened tolerance for both emotional distress and disrespectful treatment. I began to internalize the notion that my emotions were a burden to others, leading me to prioritize their comfort over my own.

This journey of emotional self-preservation shaped my interactions and relationships. It often found me in a state of disconnection, wrestling with the challenge of reconciling my innate need for vulnerability with the urge to protect myself from further pain and rejection.

Unfortunately, my upbringing positioned me as an ideal target for predators. Compounded by the antiquated teachings I received, just as many of us had during that time. I was warned against being a "tattle-tale" and instructed to follow adults without question. Questioning an adult's authority was often seen as disrespectful. Thus, I found myself in a tangled web of fear and compliance. I vividly remember my first encounter with one of the most traumatic experiences of my life.

An adult sexually abused me. The emotional turmoil of being abused by an authority figure who should have been a protector left an indelible mark on my psyche, making it clear just how misplaced trust can lead to deep-lasting trauma. I have come to realize that while instilling respect for elders is a fundamental value, it is equally vital to empower our children with the knowledge and tools they need to navigate situations where an elder may act inappropriately, disrespectfully, or in a way that makes the child uncomfortable.

Teaching children respect and a healthy level of obedience is crucial, but this must be complemented by creating an environment where they feel safe and supported in expressing their feelings. We should encourage open conversations about boundaries and personal comfort, equipping our children with the understanding that not all actions by an elder are acceptable, even if the elder is highly regarded.

Discussing specific scenarios and appropriate responses is essential to help our children feel confident in addressing their concerns. By fostering this balance, we should uphold respect and advocate for our children's emotional well-being and autonomy.

This predator found a way to exploit my vulnerability and ultimately became the cause of my deep-seated fear I now harbor about disappointing those I love. He would often corner me or approach me under the cover of darkness, when I was most defenseless, gently stirring me from my slumber on the bottom bunk. His voice, laced with a false sense of tenderness, would pierce the night's silence as he whispered, "I just need someone to love me." Those words, deceptively simple yet profoundly manipulative, hung heavy in the air.

For a child described by everyone as sensitive and emotional, such a plea became a twisted form of emotional coercion. It was during these moments, wrapped in confusion and fear, that he would make his inappropriate move, shattering my innocence and embedding a deep-rooted anxiety within me about failing to meet the expectations of those I cared for.

Regrettably, my childhood was tainted by the presence of several predators, extending beyond the one who first inflicted harm upon me. I had the painful experience of encountering four men who exploited their power and used manipulation during my formative years. While I mustered the courage to expose the first predator, the one whose actions profoundly shaped my early experiences, please understand that I didn't do it for my own sake.

At just 14 years old, I distinctly remember feeling a sense of responsibility; so, I chose to come forward to safeguard a younger relative from his relentless bullying, terrorizing, and emotional manipulation. The weight of the other three predators lingered in silence, concealed by my desire to protect those I loved. I worried that if my family discovered the truth about the horrors I faced, it would only lead to more pain and suffering for them.

A burden I refused to expose any of my loved ones to anymore. This inner conflict left me feeling like I was wearing a neon "Kick me" sign on my back, inviting further harm. Gradually, I began to internalize the blame; perhaps I was somehow responsible, maybe I was doing something to invite this abusive behavior into my life. Thoughts spiraled in my mind: Who would believe me? Would they dismiss my pain as mere childish exaggeration? My experience of exposing my first abuser stifled my voice and encouraged me to lock away my truth.

I find it strikingly unjust that a child who has endured abuse is often required to present undeniable evidence, to be articulate and persuasive in recounting their traumatic experiences, and to maintain a flawless history devoid of any mischief or harmless fibs. In stark contrast, an adult perpetrator, who may carry a lifetime of poor choices, deceitful behavior, and manipulative actions, faces no such scrutiny. A mere denial, "I didn't do it.", or a well-crafted lie can easily overshadow the pain, fear, and shame etched within the eyes of a child. This disparity highlights the harsh reality of childhood trauma, where my vulnerability had to navigate a maze of complete disbelief and skepticism, while those who inflicted harm evaded accountability with little more than a fleeting excuse.

The traumas I experienced during early childhood had ingrained in me the belief that love and abuse could coexist, leading to a distorted understanding of love long before I reached adulthood. As a young adult, I found myself consumed by anger and often overwhelmed by intense feelings of rage, particularly when my attempts to cultivate love through physical connections fell short. Seemingly trivial actions or words from potential partners could trigger explosive reactions, as I equated an intimate or physical relationship with unconditional love and expected my partner to reciprocate in ways, I had always imagined love would manifest. However, the stark reality was that I didn't love them, nor did they love me. I was navigating relationships without a clear sense of my own identity; and my desires and needs had long been suppressed.

Throughout my formative years, I focused on meeting expectations and satisfying others' needs, often at the expense of loving and understanding myself. In this chaotic emotional landscape, I felt helpless and anxious, constantly questioning whether my efforts to fulfill someone else's needs were enough to earn me a meaningful place in their heart—a sense of worthiness that would assure me of their love and respect.

Navigating the dating scene, losing my first child, and the brokenness that plagued my first marriage only deepened the wounds I carried from my past. In my late twenties, I sought therapy, which served as a crucial step in my healing journey. It helped me articulate my experiences as a child without the weight of shame, which acted as a gateway for me to confront my triggers and accept that I was not responsible for the pain I had endured. However, true forgiveness remained elusive for me and others, taking several more years of introspection and growth to cultivate.

In addition to enduring the harsh criticism of being labeled as emotional and sensitive—labels that left me feeling both dismissed and fundamentally flawed—all while being faced with abuse and manipulation at the hands of adult men, who, rather than taking the opportunity to protect and nurture me, choose to inflicted mental and physical harm. There was also a sense of servitude that marked my upbringing; I was often relegated to the role of a flunky, called upon to perform menial tasks that seemed trivial yet weighed heavily on my developing psyche.

In spite of all the work and progress made, I still find myself struggling to break the cycles of old habits that led to the creation of unhealthy relationships as well as establishing and maintaining boundaries that would safeguard my emotional well-being. I have to be conscious when practicing self-awareness and assertiveness to ensure that lay the groundwork for healthier interactions and a more fulfilling life. The challenge of unlearning deeply ingrained patterns has proven to be an ongoing journey that I am determined to work on continuously.

As a flunky, I can recall being summoned to refresh someone's drink or compelled to change the channel on the television—a task made more cumbersome in an era when remotes were not yet commonplace. At first glance, this behavior might appear typical in many households, where children help with chores. However, when viewed through the lens of the predatory grooming I was subjected to in the shadows of my family's everyday life, the situation takes on a darker significance.

As I stated before, I grew up in an environment where a child expressing an opinion or saying "no" was often interpreted as disrespectful. No matter what I was engaged in, my choices were secondary; the desires of the adults around me always took precedence, even when they were fully capable of fulfilling their own needs. As I transitioned into adulthood, I struggled to communicate my feelings and assert my needs.

My understanding of love was distorted and rooted in the belief that my worth would be measured by my willingness to meet others' needs. Consequently, refusing to comply with their expectations became a daunting challenge, as I feared the potential of being punished by adults and ostracized by my peers.

I find it incredibly fascinating how generational teachings, combined with traumatic childhood experiences, can lead to the development of harmful coping mechanisms. These mechanisms often perpetuate cycles of trauma that can last for decades. I also find it perplexing that society encourages us to believe the best course is to leave the past behind, as if we can erase our memories and emotions. Why do we accept the notion that we can selectively remember specific experiences while disregarding others, especially those that trigger negative emotions or anxiety?

The truth is, our memories are not easily compartmentalized; they shape our identities and influence our behaviors. So, instead of forgetting my past, I decided that I should do some self-evaluation and focus on cultivating healthier coping strategies. Which involved setting clear, healthy boundaries—with myself and others—and acknowledging the realities of our emotional landscapes.

It's was essential for me to foster an environment of understanding and compassion, recognizing that everyone carries their burdens of trauma, insecurities, and anxiety. By embracing this shared human experience, I was able to navigate my struggles gracefully.

At times it seemed hard to maintain but a persistent whisper insisted that I must be the change I wish to see. It remains a formidable journey, with some days presenting insurmountable challenges. There are moments when I find it incredibly difficult to assert my boundaries, to say no, or to pursue what I genuinely believe is best for my well-being. I feel anxious when I gather the courage to express my feelings, at times only to be met with distance, anger, or frustration from those I hold dear. And I began to feel a wave emotions accompanied by and undercurrent of self-blame, and I find myself fighting with emotions that threaten to pull me under. In those drowning moments, I have learned to pause, take a deep breath, and remind myself of a crucial truth: my healing journey isn't about erasing the echoes of my past. Those echoes are woven into the very fabric of who I am. Instead, my goal is to cultivate a new way of navigating the remnants of that pain, so that I no longer allow it to dictate my habits or reactions and instead I aspire to embrace myself and others with patience and grace, fostering an environment where understanding can blossom. That is how I plan to empowered myself to keep pushing forward.

In the darkness of loss. The loss of my childhood innocence, my identity, my daughter, my marriage, my family, and my mother, I had to find a way to honor the good memories, to celebrate the life of my daughter and my mother, to keep their spirits alive. I had to find a way to heal, to rebuild, and to rediscover my sense of purpose even when the world around me didn't understand.

Chapter 3
Pretender

The fear of confrontation and the anxiety surrounding how others might react will always loom large. What if they respond with anger or disappointment? My mind goes back and forth with these questions whenever I need to say no, disagree, or question someone close to me. This trepidation is another trauma response that I traced back to my early childhood experiences. When I chose to stand up for myself and confront the abuse head-on, I faced harsh ostracism; adults I trusted and respected branded me a liar. That experience was pivotal in shaping my understanding of communication and vulnerability.

That experience left me deeply wounded, and from that I learned to project an image of outward positivity and cheerfulness, masking the turmoil within. It's why I never spoke up again against an abuser of any kind.

This facade served multiple purposes: it allowed me to avoid placing what I perceived as burdens on others, helped me fit into societal norms and expectations, and, most importantly, shielded me from potential conflict. But this coping mechanism took a severe toll on my mental health. By consistently denying my true feelings and suppressing my concerns, I inadvertently created a breeding ground for anxiety, stress, and depression. It became evident that while my efforts to maintain harmony might have seemed beneficial at the time, they only led me farther away from authenticity and true happiness.

The struggle to express my feelings openly while maintaining a facade of strength left me yearning for genuine connections, yet fearful of the closeness I craved. Thus, I navigated the complexities of relationships with a cautious heart, striving to find a balance that often felt elusive, caught between the desire to "be seen" for who I truly was and the instinct to shield myself from emotional turmoil.

Before my first marriage, I had never managed to maintain a romantic relationship for more than a year. I often grew increasingly angry and frustrated when the warmth of love failed to blossom from the physical encounters, and the relationship would end. My emotional fulfillment seemed tied to these moments, and when they didn't translate into deeper feelings, I would spiral into an emotional rage of dissatisfaction.

In my attempts to forge a genuine romantic connection, I meticulously observed my love interests- their likes and dislikes, their daily habits, and the hobbies that brought them joy because I thought that if I could reshape and mold my personality and preferences to align with theirs, I would appear more lovable and deserving of their affection. My focus on adapting to their frameworks often left me feeling like I was losing a part of myself. Yet, I clung to the hope that this transformation would foster the emotional intimacy I desperately sought.

By the time I crossed paths with my first husband, I had finally reached a pivotal moment in my life – a moment when I felt ready to unearth and share the childhood traumas that had long been my silent companions. I held onto the belief that by confiding in him, I would receive the understanding and compassion I so desperately sought. I imagined a safe space where he would handle my emotional triggers with the delicacy and care they deserved, like fragile glass in a world that often felt too harsh.

Yet, as it turned out, my hopes were once again elusive, like shadows that slip through your fingers. My heartfelt confessions and anguished pleas for a deeper emotional connection fell on deaf ears, met instead with dismissal. I found myself tragically labeled as insecure and overly sensitive, a label that clung to me and deepened the chasm of isolation I already felt.

In the early days, I failed to consider the weight of his own pain, the specters of his past traumas, and how they might shape his responses to my raw vulnerability. So instead of fostering understanding, we inadvertently became each other's triggers, carelessly pushing buttons intertwined with one another's histories. In those moments, we were locked in a dance of misunderstanding, neither of us pausing to reflect on the emotional baggage we carried or the unsaid needs that lingered just beneath the surface. The truth is, had he taken a moment to ask me, I'm not entirely sure I could have articulated my needs, as lost as I was in the complexity of my own emotions.

As we both spent years pulling each other's proverbial trigger, the stakes were continually getting higher and higher. I wasn't just his girlfriend; I was a wife and a mother, and for me, the thought of walking away became more complex. I found myself caught in a web of emotions, torn between love, fear, and frustration. Each time I mustered the courage to initiate a conversation about ending our relationship—a conversation laden with the gravity of our shared lives—I was met with promises of change. Initially, the changes would seem promising, resembling the dawn of hope: for a month or two, he would make an effort, and there were moments when I allowed myself to believe things might improve. Yet as quickly as the warmth emerged, it would dissipate, leaving me alone once more with the familiar sense of distance, equipped only with my unfulfilled desire for the emotional intimacy I craved.

In the depths of my heart, I struggled with a sense of inadequacy, haunted by the fear that I could not navigate life successfully with two children in tow. I lacked the essential tools to steer through the volatile sea of my circumstances. Since I didn't believe I could do it alone, I selfishly sought solace and fulfillment outside the confines of my marriage. I found it momentarily, but it felt fleeting and ultimately unearned. When that single source of emotional nourishment withered away, I instinctively reached for another, a cycle I can't help but reflect upon with deep regret. This chapter of my life remains etched in my memory as one of the most painful and disappointing because by this point, I was a full-fledged pretender.

I wanted so badly for someone to safeguard my emotions—to wrap me in a cocoon of security and love—because, at that time, I didn't possess the ability to extend that to myself. My feelings of regret weren't rooted in the belief that I hadn't fought hard enough for them, but stemmed from my painful acknowledgment that I allowed my fears of inadequacy and my struggling sense of self-worth to lead me so far astray from who I truly am, instead of just walking away when I first realized we could not give each other what the other needed.

Ending a marriage is a complicated endeavor, far from straightforward. How I wish I could rewind the clock, choosing the nobler path instead of the duplicitous mask I wore—pretending that everything was harmonious between us while harboring pain and secrets. My desperation to be understood clouded my judgment. It made me believe that I could teach a partner how to love me by demonstrating love through the only twisted lens I had, unfortunately, seen love reflected in. I spent decades clinging to this misguided approach, and the emotional wreckage I was causing him, myself, and our family is something I will always regret.

Unfortunately, in those last few years, I held on out of fear, choosing to wear a mask of false contentment while I was actually struggling, which achieved absolutely nothing meaningful. It put me in the company of individuals whose intentions were not in my best interest, leaving me more vulnerable to interactions that lack sincerity and support.

This realization has helped me change how I evaluate my own worth. I will forever be the loving, sensitive, and emotional woman I have always been underneath all of the pain and trauma. But now I understand that I cannot help someone else cultivate a skill that I have yet to develop within myself.

As a child, I lacked the mental, physical, and emotional tools necessary to make a "Man" feel loved romantically, but my abuser convinced me that it was something I could provide. And when I entered into marriage with my first husband, I found myself unequipped for the demands and complexities of a committed relationship, just as I struggled through most of my adult life, too. It wasn't until I reached my mid to late thirties that I began to understand the importance of loving, honoring, and respecting myself as an essential foundation for any healthy connection with others.

Not having cultivated this sense of self-worth and understanding. I was unable to share the love I so desperately wanted to give, as I did not possess it for myself. This realization highlighted the gaps in my emotional development. In the shadows of my struggle, I wore a mask of indifference. When I faced abuse, I feigned strength, hiding the hurt beneath a façade of calm. When others labeled me as too emotional or overly sensitive, I brushed it off, pretending their words rolled off my back. People saw my kindness as an invitation to take advantage of me; they didn't recognize my deep hunger for love and acceptance, nor my desire to make others feel valued. Little by little, my pain shaped me into a master pretender, a performer always on stage, desperate to play the role of the strong, unaffected soul.

Chapter 4

Auto Pilot

For far too long, I endured, rationalized, and accepted disrespect as a norm in my life. I tiptoed around emotional landmines, careful not to upset anyone, fearing that the moment I spoke up, those I cared about would walk away. I found myself settling for the bare minimum, convincing myself that this was all I deserved. My mind became a battleground, conditioned to believe that tolerating such behavior was a testament to my loyalty and commitment. I thought that remaining silent in the face of disrespect somehow elevated my character, branding me as a "good" person. Yet, inside, I felt increasingly diminished, trapped in a cycle of unworthiness.

Navigating the complexities of relationships with those who overstepped my boundaries has been an enormous challenge. In moments of offense—whether from hurtful words or thoughtless actions—I often retreated into isolation. This self-imposed withdrawal only fueled my tendency to overthink and spiral into stress. I've come to realize that being a good person does not equate to silently enduring suffering; and I must dismantle the damaging association between kindness and being a doormat.

Years have slipped by while I lived on autopilot, a mere spectator in my own life. In my quest to maintain an outward façade of composure, I gradually lost sight of my true self, morphing into someone I believed others wanted me to be. Once again, this struggle traced back to my childhood, at around the age of seven when the abuse first began. It was then that my identity started to fade, overshadowed by the oppressive clouds of fear and panic that accompanied a constant fight for survival. I found myself inexplicably drawn to individuals who reflected my own internal turmoil, mirroring the negative perceptions I held of myself. Each interaction echoed the invisible scars of my past, compelling me to confront a painful truth: I had been living in a shadow of someone I was never meant to become.

I felt an overwhelming urgency to liberate myself from the relentless tension that came from existing in a perpetual state of survival mode, where every emotion felt muted and suppressed. The journey towards this release proved to be a fragile process.

In the early stages, I found myself acutely sensitive to my triggers, each one a sharp reminder of my struggles. There were moments when I could feel a rising tide of agitation within me, bubbling up as I suppressed my own feelings to ensure others felt at ease.

Each instance of mistreatment became a puzzle I tried to solve, questioning myself relentlessly and searching for clues to understand what I might have done to provoke such behavior. My long-standing tendencies as a people pleaser often left me drowning in a whirlwind of emotions: I fought back tears that threatened to spill over, burdened by guilt for simply needing a moment of solitude. Each encounter filled me with a growing sense of nervousness and anxiety, as I wrestled with the daunting task of processing how the words and actions of others were affecting me.

To navigate this challenging terrain, I realized I needed to create a significant distance between myself and these emotional landmines. It was important for me to step back and observe my experiences from a safer vantage point, allowing myself the necessary time to develop a clearer understanding of my feelings and discover healthier ways to move forward.

I found myself at a crossroads, a moment that compelled me to truly examine who I had become. It was a revelation that struck deep—recognizing that I had morphed into my own greatest obstacle. This acknowledgment does not at all imply that I needed to shoulder the blame for every misfortune; rather, it was crucial for me to accept and understand the significant role I played in my own narrative.

I was the sole architect of my existence, and it became abundantly clear that I had to reclaim my life from the clutches of autopilot. I could no longer engage in a relentless struggle for a life that felt increasingly constricting, nor could I maintain the facade that everything was perfectly fine. I sensed the need to cultivate an honest and genuine trust that, despite appearances, everything would ultimately fall into place—even when circumstances felt overwhelming.

Transitioning off autopilot was an arduous task; it felt chaotic and raw, and I struggled with a gnawing fear of alienating those I hold dear. Nevertheless, I pressed onward, courageously embracing the swirling uncertainty that accompanied my journey. I navigated through spells of loneliness and faced the painful reality of losing individuals I had once believed would stand by my side until the very end. Yet, with each step forward, I began to forge a new path, one that was uniquely mine, rich with the complexities of change and growth.

In the depths of life's uncertainty, to a radiant light bursting with possibilities. When I found myself at an emotional rock bottom, a place devoid of hope and clarity, I made the climactic decision to bet on myself. With every beat of my heart, I chose to trust in my own resilience, even though the future loomed uncertain and shrouded in mystery.

It was in that moment of introspection, that I inhaled deeply, feeling the cool air fill my lungs, I closed my eyes, surrendering to the silence around me. My mother's voice reverberated in my mind like a guiding star through the shadows: “Chel, you are capable of handling whatever life throws your way; trust yourself.” her words were a warm embrace, anchoring me in the chaos. At that instant, I felt the weight of auto-pilot lift, and I could sense the stirring of a newfound strength within me. I was ready to face the unknown, emboldened by the belief that I could navigate whatever storms lay ahead.

No more pretending, no more coasting through life on auto-pilot. I'm done with blame, shame, and guilt. It's all about genuine acceptance now—accepting myself, accepting others, and embracing the world as it is. It's time to shed the mask and show up authentically as ME! Ready to live out my purpose with confidence and clarity.

Part Two: The Purpose

"For I know the plans I have for you, plans to prosper you and not to harm you, plans to give you hope and a future."

-Jeremiah 29:11

Chapter 5

Flawsome

Flawed? Absolutely! Broken? Without a doubt. There's a strong possibility that I could shatter into countless pieces once more. Am I worthy? Yes, I firmly believe I am still deserving of love and grace. Each day, I embark on a journey of self-discovery, learning to embrace my imperfections. I am continually filled with gratitude, recognizing that despite my struggles, God chooses to hold me together, weaving my fragmented self into a tapestry of resilience and hope.

There is no flawless version of ourselves, yet there exists the potential for a more refined and enriched version. The choices we make shape our identity, and to transform into something different, we must dare to make choices that can lead us toward growth. Each day that God grants us the gift of waking up is a reminder that our journey of self-discovery is ongoing; the person we are destined to become is still a work in progress.

That's why I have made a conscious decision to embrace change, striving to be different, regardless of the paths I have trodden in the past. Life unfolds like a winding road, devoid of turn-by-turn directions, and now I find a certain joy in this uncertainty. Some of my most cherished memories have blossomed along the unexpected detours. unscripted moments, the ones that veer off the beaten path, where I discovered laughter, adventure, and a deeper understanding of what it means to truly live.

Observing my mother in her final days imparted an unexpected yet profoundly valuable lesson. In those moments, nobody lingered over her flaws, quirks, or past mistakes. There was no emphasis placed on her achievements, the wealth she accumulated, or her physical beauty.

Instead, what emerged as truly significant was the depth of her influence in our lives. We found ourselves reflecting on the boundless love and care she selflessly offered to friends and family. It was the warmth of her spirit, the unwavering support she provided, and the countless memories woven from her kindness that held the greatest value. Her legacy wasn't defined by tangible accomplishments but rather by the profound impact she had on our hearts and lives.

I have come to deeply appreciate the beauty of being flawed. Each day, as I awaken to the blessings of life, I realize I have the power to confront and transform the imperfections that I carry—whether they be in my character, my actions, or my attitudes. It isn't uncommon for me to stumble or make mistakes; these experiences, though challenging, are essential components of the human experience.

As I navigate through life, I find that the courage to try again, despite the setbacks, is what truly defines me. When the time comes for me to stand before God at the end of my journey, my deepest wish is to do so with a heart full of gratitude and a spirit that has sought to utilize every gift and opportunity placed before me. My goal is to strive relentlessly to become the best version of myself, aiming to fulfill the purpose I believe has been instilled in me. This commitment to self-improvement and service to God is how I hope to honor the life I have been given.

Embracing the concept of being Flawsome involves a valuable self-reflection process that fosters humility and growth. It's essential to explore the reasons behind my thoughts, words, and actions. This journey demands a deep love for myself, empowering me to prioritize the respect and care I truly deserve. In this transformative process, I realized that it was necessary to shift my focus away from simply being perceived as a "good" person and instead embrace the more authentic path of becoming a Flawsome individual.

As I took this time for self-reflection, I realized it was crucial to identify which trauma responses needed my immediate attention. The first on my list was people-pleasing. I knew it was time to set clear boundaries and focus on investing in relationships where the effort was mutual. I wanted to break free from the cycle of overextending myself just to receive the bare minimum in return. I craved connections that felt balanced and reciprocal.

Not because I craved the act of giving to receive, but rather to improve my ability to set boundaries and limitations in a safe environment. I could barely utter the word "NO," so I wanted to seek out spaces where a refusal would not result in a painful farewell. I longed to escape the kind of misunderstandings that could escalate into explosive confrontations where only the lowest blows were permitted. I needed to be in environments infused with generous spirits of grace and understanding—a haven where I could express my thoughts freely, unburdened by the weight of judgment or the anxiety of being subjected to relentless scrutiny. In such nurturing environments, I hoped to find solace in open dialogue, fostering connections that were built on empathy and trust.

Another significant trauma response I needed to address

was my tendency to harshly evaluate myself and get trapped in a whirlwind of overthinking. I started reminding myself to take a step back and not let emotional reactions take control. I learned that the words and actions of others often stem from their own unresolved issues and personal growth journeys, rather than being a reflection of my worth. Embracing this perspective has been a game-changer, guiding me toward healthier relationships and a kinder self-image. The reason for this approach is to enhancing mental control rather than attempting to influence the behavior of others. It involved addressing self-doubt and negative self-talk, with an emphasis on undertaking a mental cleanse to eliminate unnecessary clutter from the mind. The goal was to adopt more positive and gracious thoughts.

There is dignity in acknowledging one's imperfections. When you can fully embrace your flaws and confront your own truth—despite the pain and heartache that may have accompanied your journey—it becomes a powerful testament to your resilience. I take immense pride in my ability to persevere. Through this journey, I've realized that my strength lies not in perfection but in my courage in facing my imperfections.

While I still find myself reflecting on the moments that broke me, and there are times when those memories bring tears, I have learned to be grateful for those broken pieces. They have contributed fundamentally to my identity and growth. This beautiful complexity is what makes me "Flawsome"—a blend of flaws and awesomeness that defines my humanity and the depth of my experience. Each scar tells a story of struggle and survival, and I embrace every part of that narrative.

Chapter 6

Grace, Growth, Gratitude

I can easily fill my days with memories of the pain others have inflicted upon me. Each moment lingers, a collection of experiences that have shaped my understanding of trust and betrayal. Those instances resonate deeply—friends who turned their backs, words that cut like knives, and the unfulfilled promises that loomed large. Yet, as I sift through these memories, I realize that this reflection would be woefully one-sided if I did not also confront the times, I have caused pain to others.

Those moments when my shortcomings show up often stand out just as starkly: the harsh words spoken in frustration, the indifference shown when someone needed me the most, and the moments when my own insecurities blinded me to the needs of those I love. Acknowledging these flaws is not easy, but it is a crucial part of my journey. It forces me to confront my imperfect nature and accept that I have contributed to the very cycle of hurt I so often speak of.

Through this dual reckoning, I find a deeper understanding of my own growth and maturation. Each painful encounter, whether received or given, has served as a foundation for learning and evolving. I've come to recognize that humanity is stitched together by a common thread of imperfection. We all stumble, make mistakes, and sometimes hurt those we care about without intending to. It is in this recognition that I find solace—knowing that I am not alone in my struggles, nor is anyone else. We all crave grace and forgiveness. However, the very act of extending these gifts can be so difficult, especially when we carry our own burdens of hurt and disappointment.

Taking time to reflecting on my past taught me that healing comes not from merely forgetting the pain but from understanding its significance in shaping who I am. It requires a conscious effort to recognize our shared imperfections and to offer compassion to both ourselves and others. In this journey, I discovered that the true essence of grace lies in our ability to see beyond our wounds and reach for connection, transforming our painful experiences into lessons of love and empathy. So, I offer those I have hurt a sincere apology, not with the expectation of being forgiven, but as a heartfelt acknowledgment of my shortcomings. My words flow from a genuine place of remorse, an earnest desire to mend the pain I've inadvertently inflicted on others. In this act of humility, I seek to illuminate the shadows of my past actions, recognizing that they may have echoed deeper wounds in those I affected.

This apology is a bridge, built from my understanding of the impact of my behavior, however unwittingly done, and it symbolizes my commitment to growth. Each syllable carries the weight of reflection; I recall the moments when my choices hurt others, even when my intentions were not malicious. The stirring into my soul serves as a reminder that to truly grow, one must own their actions and bear their consequences, however uncomfortable that may be.

As I express these thoughts, I consider how they might resonate in the hearts of those I've hurt. I hope it brings them a flicker of solace—some amount of relief for the wounds I inflicted as I honor their feelings. Each apology is layered with the understanding that healing takes time, and my mere words might not suffice to repair the damage done. My journey of offering apologies intertwines with my own process of self-forgiveness. I recognize that just as I extend grace to others, I am challenged to extend it to myself as well. I confront the tendencies to dwell in guilt and shame, realizing that I am deserving of compassion—just as I wish to extend it to those I've hurt. It is a delicate dance between acknowledging past failures and allowing myself the space to grow beyond them.

In this reflective space, I find strength in vulnerability. Each apology I offer is not a sign of weakness but rather an acknowledgment of our shared humanity. It conveys that we all stumble and cannot be defined solely by our mistakes. I am constantly striving to nurture my spirit and foster an environment where healing can flourish. I stride forward with a renewed sense of purpose, understanding that the journey towards genuine connection requires both courage and humility. It is my intention to remain open-hearted, fostering relationships built on mutual respect, empathy, and a commitment to understanding. This desire for connection fuels my willingness to apologize, to forgive, and to continue evolving into a better version of myself—as someone who embraces the complexities of life with grace and compassion.

Grace has allowed me to outgrow many things in my life. I have moved beyond the unrealistic expectations that others have placed on me. I have let go of people who wear masks and secretly rejoice in my misfortunes. I refuse to shrink myself for men who feel intimidated by my emotional intelligence and kind nature. I have outgrown those who cannot celebrate my achievements. I no longer try to please everyone, and I have moved past society's pressures to be perfect and emotionless. I have outgrown anything and anyone that does not enrich my soul.

This task is one that requires consistency and will remain a work in progress. Allow me to explain, in a whirlwind of just a few years, my life unraveled in ways I never could have imagined. I went through a heart-wrenching divorce that tore my family apart, leaving emotional scars that would take time to heal. As I navigated the turbulent waters of separation, I faced a relentless onslaught of bad relationships (I use that word relationship loosely) and financial struggles. Selling my house felt like surrendering a piece of my past—each room held echoes of laughter, love, and countless memories I made with my children, was reduced to an empty shell.

Amid these upheavals, I stood by helplessly as my mother took her final breaths. Watching her pass away was a living nightmare, an ache that burrowed deep into my soul. Just as I thought I might catch a break, more financial troubles emerged, each new challenge like a wave crashing over me. And as if the universe hadn't tested me enough, I found myself in an unforgiving battle with cancer, each day a struggle against an invisible foe trying to maintain a courageous smile on my face. With all this weighing on me, I often felt trapped in a cycle of despair, as if I were walking through quicksand, unable to take a step forward. Whenever people felt compelled to dissect my every move—whenever my choices didn't align with their narrow expectations—it felt like daggers piercing my already wounded spirit.

In response, I made a conscious choice. I decided to sit silently, a practiced smile on my face, and endure the criticism with grace. I swore I would not let anyone push me into tarnishing my character, as I had allowed others to do in the past. I knew that if I were to snap, to lash out in anger or seek revenge, that would become the defining moment of my story. Just as it had in my first marriage the myriad struggles that had toughened my spirit would fade from memory, overshadowed by a single, rash reaction. So, I clung to my self-control like a lifeline, determined to rise above the turmoil without losing the essence of who I am. I wanted to emerge from this haunting chapter not only as a survivor but as a testament to the strength and integrity that can arise even from the depths of despair.

With this new found clarity, I summoned the courage to confront my own excuses—each one a small chain that bound me to mediocrity. I recognized that I could no longer be the architect of my own discontent. My journey was fueled by a resolute commitment to prioritize my own needs, to cultivate a nurturing space for my emotional and mental well-being, and to foster a mindset that not only embraced growth but danced joyfully with the possibilities of life. I was ready to reclaim my narrative, to step boldly into the light, and to stop allowing discouragement to dictate my path.

The truth is that the process really feels like a rollercoaster ride. One day, I find myself in a state of peace, overflowing with motivation and genuinely in love with the person I'm evolving into. I experience a deep sense of gratitude for every challenge and lesson that has brought me to this point in my life. However, out of nowhere, the next moment can plunge me into a whirlwind of emotions. I become tearful, grappling with self-anger for enduring so much hardship. It's as if I can't get anything right, and an overwhelming exhaustion washes over me, threatening to pull me under. Yet through all the ups and downs, I consciously choose to keep pushing forward. I remind myself that this struggle is part of the journey, and somehow, that keeps me grounded and motivated to continue.

Surrounding myself with the right people has also been a transformative experience, allowing me to navigate life's roller-coaster of emotions without the burden of judgment. I remarried the summer of twenty-twenty four and my husband has been my steadfast companion throughout this journey, and it's hard to believe that when I first embarked on this chaotic path, we were not even engaged, let alone married. He stood by me, ready to listen to my deepest fears and harshest truths, never flinching or changing the subject to draw attention to his own struggles. Instead, he offered a safe space for my vulnerability, welcoming my pain without a hint of discomfort.

In his presence, I felt a profound sense of acceptance, a reassurance that it was okay to be raw and real. He acknowledged the harsh realities of life while simultaneously celebrating its beauty, deftly balancing both in a way that made me feel understood.

With him, I discovered a sanctuary where I could be my true self—where my emotions could swirl freely, unfiltered and unrestrained. In his embrace, I found a place where my heart, mind, and body could coexist in harmony. This love—a blend of support, acceptance, and understanding—has allowed me to shed the layers of pretense I once wore. I was finally able to embrace my authentic self, liberated too simply be me.

The freedom that comes with accepting imperfections—like walking around with a stain on my shirt—profoundly resonates with me. I've come to celebrate my quirks and my individuality, letting the rhythm of my own drum guide my decisions.

Mistakes are now seen as invaluable lessons rather than failures to hide. Understanding that everyone stumbles has given me the courage to share my missteps; I am not alone in this human experience. I've learned to tune out the judgment and criticism that can often come from those closest to you. I recognize now that many reactions stem from each persons' own fears and insecurities, which can reshape their views on their choices and the choices of others. The struggle to make decisions that might upset others or go against societal norms is a challenge I now face with confidence. In the realm of relationships, I strive to show love and support when my friends and family wrestle with their own tough decisions. It's important to me that they know I am here for them, just as I wish to be supported in my own journey. I embrace the complexities of life and relationships, choosing connection over criticism and compassion over conformity.

Growth, for me, truly began when I made the decision to turn inward and spend some quality time with myself. I realized that in order to embark on the journey of healing, I had to navigate through my own emotional landscape without dragging anyone else into my turmoil. The concept of growth evolved into something deeper and more meaningful; it required me to seek professional guidance and to shed the fears that had long held me back from stepping into my own power. I began to embrace my highest self with confidence and without reservation, fully aware of the importance of this profound transformation.

As I delved into this self-discovery process, I committed to a path of self-reflection and accountability. I made it a priority to check my thoughts and actions, recognizing when I was slipping into old habits of blaming others for my circumstances. Instead, I took ownership of my life, understanding that my journey was uniquely mine to navigate. The realization washed over me that I could no longer harbor resentment towards those around me who were simply prioritizing their own well-being. Now understanding that it is essential for me to prioritize my own needs, even if that meant redefining or stepping away from relationships that had once held great significance in my life. Growth isn't always comfortable, but I knew that embracing it was vital for my personal evolution.

Lord, I am grateful! I know who you are, and in turn, I now know who I am. God, guided me through the darkest nights, becoming a beacon that illuminated my soul when I felt lost. During times when I struggled to get through each day, he was my anchor, holding me together as my world seemed to crumbled around me. I once believed that I had nothing left to give, but then, in a moment of divine revelation, God unveiled an entire galaxy of strength and potential within me.

Gratitude became a powerful catalyst, unlocking doors I never knew existed. It transformed the little I had into a sense of abundance, overflowing with possibilities. Where there was once denial, I found acceptance; chaos morphed into order, and confusion sharpened into clarity. There are still and there will always be challenges but gratitude has been the thread that wove my house into a genuine home, in spite of. Gratitude has enriched my understanding of my past, leading me to a place of inner peace and a profound sense of purpose that guides me forward.

Once I discovered grace, I realized that all my mistakes had severed my sense of purpose. It became clear to me how easily one can lose their way, especially when burdened by the weight of regret and self-doubt. I never want a child or young person to suffer for years without an empathetic ear and a caring heart to help guide them through despair. Everyone deserves support, especially during their formative years when they're trying to understand the world around them.

Deep down, I believe we all find ourselves wrestling with life's challenges that go beyond mere solutions or quick fixes; we crave genuine connection that foster understanding. We don't always want to be "fixed" or "saved" in the conventional sense. Instead, what really matter is to being truly seen— to have someone look past the surface and recognize the intricate layers of our experience.

We want our thoughts and feelings to resonate with another human-being, to be heard without judgment or receive a rushed response of some unauthentic surface level advice. In those moments of despair, it's the simple comfort of companionship that we long for, a reminder that we are not alone in our struggles. It's in that yearning; we discover the transformative power of empathy. It became clear to me that my true desire is for a shared human experience, one that affirms my existence and validate my emotions. I wanted to know that my pain mattered, and that there are others who understand what it felts like to be lost or overwhelmed, and that I am not navigating these turbulent waters alone. This realization became the cornerstone of my own healing journey.

As for gratitude, expressing gratitude is a simple and powerful tool that has also aided me throughout my journey.

I had taken a lot for granted and I never saw myself as that type of person. My desire for more, to have what I thought I was supposed to have given my age, education, and what others who shared similar demographics had, I couldn't appreciate what was right in front of me. I failed to recognize how fortunate I was to have even the simplest things in life. I am not sure what tangible pleasures in life you have or plan to achieve, but try to open your heart and soul to the pleasures of gratitude. Gratitude is much more than just a word it's a place you can go to sit and appreciate all that has helped you along the way. When I hear the word gratitude it brings to mind countless memories that have countered acted the bad days along the way.

Throughout my life, I've faced a variety of challenges that could easily be seen as burdens, yet intertwined with these hardships are countless beautiful memories that collectively shape my identity. For instance, I vividly recall nights spent laughing with friends, the warmth of their camaraderie illuminating even the darkest of days. It's vital to recognize that even in the midst of trials, there exists a profound reservoir of love and greatness waiting to be un-covered. The most important lesson I've learned from my experiences is the necessity of embracing not only the joyful moments but also expressing gratitude for every encounter and event both uplifting and painful. Each step of this journey, from exhilarating highs to the daunting lows, has played an integral role in shaping who I am today.

I have come to believe deeply that my existence is part of a greater plan, where my struggles aren't punishments but rather indispensable instruments in cultivating empathy and understanding for everyone around me. For example, when I faced rejection or loss, instead of seeing these as only sad moments, I began to view them as opportunities for growth. They taught me resilience and helped me forge connections with others who have walked similar paths. Just as we celebrate moments of pure joy like the birth of a child or the thrill of personal achievements it's equally essential to honor our struggles. They're not just obstacles; they're the vessels that shape our character. In my life story, both the radiant highlights and the shadows have intertwined elegantly, creating a rich tapestry of experiences that allow me to connect more deeply with others. This connection fosters a shared understanding of the complexity, beauty, and fragility of life itself. My journey reflects the notion that every moment, whether draped in light or cloaked in darkness, contributes uniquely to the person I am becoming.

Chapter 7

The Dream

Initially I embarked on this journey for myself, fueled by a burning desire for change. I was tired of feeling weighed down by dissatisfaction and yearned for a life filled with purpose. Taking full responsibility for how I chose to show up became my guiding principle. I confronted the repetitive cycles that held me captive, acknowledging when I hadn't treated myself with the respect I deserved. I became acutely aware of the negative thoughts that looped endlessly in my mind. Stepping away from the victim mentality was a pivotal moment for me. I bravely called myself out on the excuses that had been my crutch and stop letting myself down. This commitment wasn't just a shift; it was a revelation. It was the moment I decided to transform my dreams into reality, embracing the strength within me to create a life of fulfillment and joy.

When I allowed myself the freedom to dream, everything shifted. Discovering my life purpose sparked an urgency within me; I realized that true happiness and peace would elude me until I actively pursued this calling. Opening myself up to possibilities changed my life in incredible ways, leaving me exhilarated and transformed. The energy and magic within me expanded, magnifying my sense of fulfillment. Each moment spent mastering myself has been richly rewarding, leading me to a state of genuine peace and alignment with my true self.

Now, fueled by gratitude for the solace I found along the way, I feel a deep commitment to pay it forward. I aspire to create a ripple effect of compassion and understanding in both my personal life and professional endeavors. I want to build bridges of connection, where vulnerability is welcomed and where others can feel the reassurance that their struggles are shared. Whether through conversations, mentorship, or community initiatives, my goal is to provide a safe space for individuals to express their fears and hopes. By sharing my story and listening to the stories of others, I aim to cultivate an environment that celebrates authenticity and fosters resilience. It's about dismantling the walls of isolation and encouraging an open dialogue that acknowledges our shared humanity. Ultimately, I dream of helping others realize that they are never truly alone and that there is profound strength in seeking and offering understanding.

Discovering my true passions has been enriching and transformative. When I began to envision my future and the possibilities that lay ahead, I realized that I had to look beyond the conventional measures of success, such as financial gain or societal status. In doing so, I identified my dreams: at the pinnacle was my aspiration to become a doctor specializing in Clinical Mental Health (Marriage and Family Counseling). Following closely behind that ambition is my goal of becoming a college professor. The idea of sharing knowledge, guiding young minds, and engaging in meaningful academic discourse excites me. I want to inspire students to explore the intricacies of mental health, encourage them to pursue their passions, and ask the tough questions about life and humanity. I want to fully embrace my dream of becoming Dr. Robinson, regardless of the obstacles I may face or the time it may take. The importance of this mission transcends any fears associated with stepping outside my comfort zone. It is about following a path that aligns with my values and allows me to uplift and empower others through knowledge and compassion.

This career path is not merely a vocational choice; it represents the apex of my dedication to understanding the intricacies of the human mind and emotions. I am drawn to the idea of delving deep into the complexities of mental health, helping individuals untangle their emotional challenges, and guiding them toward healing and resilience. I envision myself in a clinical setting, working one-on-one with clients, employing evidence-based therapies, and creating tailored interventions that foster growth and self-awareness. Through this, I hope to make a meaningful impact in people's lives, guiding them on their journeys toward emotional well-being and a more fulfilling existence.

The most remarkable aspect of all of this has been the profound realization that, as a therapist, my path is one of continuous growth. In reflecting on my purpose and the legacy I aspire to create; I've come to understand that my quest for knowledge will always be ongoing. Learning about myself and others is a never-ending pursuit. Embracing my humanity means that I no longer need to pretend; instead, I choose to engage fully in the beautiful complexities of life, accepting both the ups and downs that come my way. For me, failure has become a grounding force, helping me remain humble and empathetic toward the struggles others face. At the same time, my victories inspire me, fueling a deep sense of optimism and courage that encourages me to uplift those around me. I want to inspire others to keep dreaming and searching for their own purpose, reminding them that every journey is unique yet interconnected.

My dreams serve as a powerful bridge, connecting the person I was, the person I am today, with the person I am destined to become. They push me to venture beyond the safety of my comfort zone and into the realm of my true potential. Although fear occasionally grips me, I understand that this anxiety signifies I'm on the brink of undertaking something courageous. So, despite the uncertainties that accompany my journey, I remain steadfast in my commitment to my dreams and my purpose. This dream of mine is not merely another box to check; it blazes like an unquenchable fire within my heart, its warmth pushing me forward while illuminating the path ahead. It serves as a constant reminder that life is meant to be more than a monotonous cycle of daily tasks. I've learned to follow the flickering light of hope within me, even on the darkest days when it seems nearly extinguished. I have had to rely on this inner radiance, trusting that it will ultimately guide me to where I am truly meant to be.

My dreams are evidence that my mind can envision realities yet untouched by my hands. They are the gentle whispers of possibility that beckon me to confront the limitations that society might impose and to boldly rewrite my own narrative. I refuse to let the magnitude of my aspirations intimidate me. Each monumental accomplishment in history began as a dream, followed by courageous strides toward the unknown. With each step I take, I am not just moving toward a goal; I am crafting a life brimming with purpose and potential.

Part Three: The Action

"Life's not about expecting, hoping, and wishing, it's about doing, being, and becoming."

– Mike Dooley

Chapter 8

Say-Less, Do More

Wishing for a brighter future and embracing hope can feel like a comforting shield against life's uncertainties. However, I've come to realize that a positive mindset, while valuable, can only carry you so far without action to back it up. To manifest the life I envision, I needed to transform my dreams into concrete steps. This transformation is not just about setting goals; it's about having the courage to pursue them relentlessly.

My journey took an unexpected turn in May 2024 when I received a cancer diagnosis. The weight of that news was heavy, transforming my world in an instant. Suddenly, my priorities shifted dramatically. I found myself at a crossroads—I had planned to dive headfirst into my graduate program, but my health had to take precedence. I needed to pause and focus on my treatments, channeling all my energy into healing.

Some of you may grasp this, but for those who do not, cancer is a relentless shadow that lingers, even when treatments conclude and the words "remission" echo in my ears. It has become an integral part of who I am; my scars reveal stories that a fleeting glance cannot begin to comprehend. The piercing pains and dull, yet persistent aches—a variety of sensation—linger long after the initial battle, remnants of the fierce struggle I endured as my body fought to heal.

The radiation treatments, though designed to eradicate the malignant cells, have left their indelible marks on my skin. My darkened skin and peculiar deformities tell a story of their own, minimal in the eyes of others but monumental in my heart. Each time I catch my reflection in the mirror, I am reminded of the horror that resided within me, the very essence of something terrible that once threatened my life. No matter how much I strive to accept and embrace these changes, they are constant reminders of the fragility of my existence; they whisper that the threat could return without warning.

Learning to live with this reality has been a complex journey, filled with an intricate dance between acceptance and fear. I look at my scars not just as marks of survival, but as symbols of resilience and transformation. They encapsulate a battle fought, a testimony to strength, and they remind me daily that while I am healing, there remains a duality within me—where the fear of recurrence lingers like a faint shadow, always just behind the light of my newfound strength.

When a doctor delivers the devastating news that you have cancer, it feels as though a heavy shadow has cast itself over your future, almost like a death sentence hanging in the air. The word "cancer" strikes an all-consuming fear deep within me, especially since both my mother and grandmother lost their battles against this disease. The terror that grips me is profound and unyielding.

Currently, I am diligently following my hormone therapy regimen, a beacon of hope in this grim landscape. However, my anxiety intensified as I recently formed a deep connection with my aunt, who, like me, is a survivor of breast cancer. Just weeks after she completed her hormone therapy, the shocking news came: her cancer had returned. This harrowing twist of fate left me feeling vulnerable and shaken, and it’s impossible for me not to feel a sense of dread about my own journey. How could I not be terrified, knowing the precariousness of this fight?

I've come to realize that during life's most challenging moments, the true nature of those who claim to care about you becomes painfully clear. It’s a revealing time; you can easily distinguish between those who remain steadfast by your side and those who choose to walk away. I'm genuinely thankful to those who decided to leave my life, as their departure created space for my personal growth in the areas they vacated. Their absence allowed the people who truly love and appreciate me to step into the spotlight, enabling me to invest more deeply in those meaningful relationships.

I've learned to accept my journey without minimizing or denying any part of it. It's perfectly acceptable to outgrow connections with those who make us feel undervalued or unwanted. As I've navigated this path, I've shifted my approach—I now speak less and take more actionable steps towards my goals and values. I've reached a significant milestone in my self-discovery, where I have a deep understanding of who I am, what I truly desire, and what I deserve from my relationships.

No longer will I compromise my worth for the sake of others. I recognize the value of my time, effort, love, and care, and I refuse to invest these precious gifts in those who do not hold them in high regard. I've arrived at a stage in my life where self-love has become paramount, outshining any external affection. Choosing myself has become a daily commitment, even when it's not supported or recognized by others. I continue to hold a deep affection for them, as well as a profound gratitude for the invaluable lessons I've gained through our shared experiences. However, I've come to realize that mere conversations alone cannot create true transformations in individuals or circumstances. It is the actions that unfold in response to both the spoken and unspoken words that truly cultivate meaningful change. This understanding has shaped how I view relationships and personal growth, emphasizing the importance of taking concrete steps rather than relying solely on dialogue.

I decided to take a step back from social media, and it was a transformative period for me. In the past, I often shared snippets of my personal challenges and the research I've been delving into. Surprisingly, the feedback I received was overwhelmingly positive, with many people resonating with my journey and insights.

However, I came to realize that in order to truly work on myself and apply the valuable lessons I've learned from my experiences, as well as the knowledge I've gained through research and the therapeutic techniques provided by my therapist, I needed to prioritize action over words. It became clear that to effectively grow, I had to shift my focus inward.

By saying less and doing more, I've created space for introspection and genuine personal development. This commitment has allowed me to concentrate on what truly matters—working diligently towards my goals, fulfilling my purpose, and taking tangible steps to turn my dreams into reality. It's been a rewarding journey of self-discovery, and I genuinely feel that this deliberate pause has set me on the right path. So, I let go, to allow myself to vibrate higher on a higher level.

Navigating this period of my life was challenging. Each day is a blend of hope and fear, punctuated by doctor's appointments and treatments. Yet amidst the struggles, I discovered an inner resilience I didn't know I possessed. Each small victory—whether it was completing a treatment session or simply having a good day—became a stepping stone, reminding me that action, no matter how incremental, can still be a powerful force.

While I delayed my academic aspirations, I approached this setback with a determination to come back stronger. I immersed myself in self-care and mental wellness, seeking out activities that brought me joy and peace. I found solace in writing, painting, and connecting with loved ones, activities that nurtured my spirit even when my body felt fragile.

As I look ahead, I embrace the belief that overcoming those hurdles was an important part of my journey. This experience has sparked a deeper understanding of what I wanted for my future, and I am committed to pursuing my dreams with renewed vigor. This chapter, though filled with challenges, is also one of growth and resilience, setting the stage for a renewed focus on my aspirations.

Chapter 9

Inhale Courage, Exhale Fear

Courage blossomed within me like a flower breaking through the rigid soil after a long winter. It emerged during a pivotal moment when the heavy burdens I had been lugging—an array of regrets, fears, and insecurities—finally began to slip away like sand through my fingers. The once unyielding chains of my past, which had held me captive for so long, crumbled into dust, allowing me to step into a bright expanse of tranquility that felt like the dawn of a new era.

In this newfound clarity, I realized an astounding truth: no matter the storms I might face, I possess an innate strength that will carry me through to the other side. The very essence of survival now felt like a promise—a promise that I could emerge stronger, like a phoenix rising from its ashes. With this perspective, the specter of failure transformed before my eyes; it became a catalyst for growth, and I found myself ready to embrace new beginnings, free from the shackles of shame.

My courage now serves as a rugged compass, guiding me through the sometimes-turbulent landscape of life. Setbacks no longer loom as a dark cloud, but instead unfurls itself as a setup for newfound triumphs. I've come to understand that life isn't merely about evading difficulties, but about soaring above them, like an eagle riding a thermal updraft, thriving and finding purpose even amongst the commotion.

Sure, there are still times I step into the arena of life unprepared, feeling the weight of uncertainty pressing against my chest. But I choose to arrive imperfectly; my voice may tremble, and my hands may shake and that's okay I give myself grace to stumble. In each misstep, I discover rich lessons hidden like treasures waiting to be unearthed. I take the time to sift through my losses, savoring the insights they offer, and I find opportunities sparkling among my failures that beckon me to learn and grow.

There's a rhythm to my journey—sometimes requiring the serenity of patience, at other times the fervor of pursuit. I recognize the necessity to linger in reflection when needed, but I also rush toward my goals with passion when the moment feels just right. The fire of motivation burns within me, ignited by the desire to live for myself. I awaken each day, courageous and free, choosing to release the unrealistic shackles of perfectionism. I allow myself to create, to craft, to explore, doing my best until I learn the nuances of refinement.

Even in writing this book, I navigated through a myriad of misadventures. With each tentative word, I learned and adapted, transforming mistakes into stepping stones that guided me toward clarity and authentic expression. This journey illuminated a profound truth: courage is not a singular event but an unfolding practice, a dance with life that embraces imperfections, cherishes growth, and confidently weaves through the fabric of my existence, reminding me that every heartbeat echoes the melody of resilience.

I have come to understand that I haven't stumbled along the wrong path or ruined my future; rather, I am deeply entrenched in the process of living out my destiny. Every hardship I have faced has been, and continues to be, a necessary part of a grand design. In those moments when fear tries to worm its way into my thoughts and my spirit feels heavy with weariness, I quickly push that darkness aside. I anchor myself in gratitude, standing tall and lifting my gaze, ready to thank God for the blessings that I know are on their way.

This journey has taught me that embracing gratitude, even in the amidst of struggle, can transform those battles into a powerful narrative of my truth. I had to shed my fears and meet each situation with an open heart, prepared to fully experience everything life offers. I chose to believe in myself, and I embarked on a quest for deeper meaning and purpose, seeking answers that resonate with my soul.

I have forgiven myself for allowing fear to shape my actions and for letting negative energies take advantage of my spirit. I lacked the understanding I have now. So, I created a purposeful action plan, placing my well-being at the forefront. One by one, I am slicing through the cords of fear that have long held me captive, and with each severed tie, my spirit feels progressively freer, lighter, and more luminous, I sense that God beams down with pride as I shatter these unhealthy patterns, creating a solid foundation for my children and their future descendants to flourish mentally, emotionally, and spiritually.

I've made space in my life as much room as I can because I see people in my family and my community struggling, and I am driven to help them find their healing. I recognize that not everyone can navigate their pain alone; for those who need extra support, I aspire to provide that strength. I want to hold their hands and accompany them through the storm, ensuring they know they are not alone on their journey to the other side.

"Enough with Fear!" I shout, embracing the courage to accept and share my truth. Life isn't merely about believing everything happens for a reason. Sometimes, we make choices that lead us astray, and it's essential to confront those decisions and grow from the experience. Happiness is not defined by the polished appearance of our homes, but by the depth of love we cultivate within those walls. True joy does not hinge on achieving success by a specific deadline but rather on discovering a passion so profound that time feels irrelevant.

Peace does not arise from seeking the world's approval; it manifests in waking each day with a sense of tranquility within oneself, unaffected by how others perceive us. Genuine happiness emerges not from possessing the best of everything but from making the most of what we have. Healing is not the outcome of resolving every issue or achieving a flawless existence; it is the understanding that the light of hope is always there, waiting for us to lift our heads and take a moment to truly see it shine.

My therapist shared a breathing technique that I've found helpful; it's centered around the idea of cultivating courage while releasing fear. Here's a detailed guide on how to practice this technique:

1. **Find a Comfortable Position**: Start by sitting or lying down in a quiet space where you won't be disturbed. Ensure your posture is relaxed yet upright.
2. **Close Your Eyes**: This can help you focus better on your breath and eliminate distractions around you.
3. **Connect with Your Breath**: Begin by taking a few moments to notice your natural breathing pattern. Feel the air entering and leaving your body without changing it.
4. **Inhale Courage**: As you breath in, visualize or think about what courage means to you. Picture it as a vibrant light, a warm energy, or a powerful force. Inhale deeply through your nose for a count of four, imagining this courage filing your lungs and spreading throughout your body.
5. **Hold Your Breath**: After inhaling, hold your breath for a count of four. During this pause, focus on the strength and positivity of the courage you've just breathed in.
6. **Exhale Fear**: Now, slowly exhale through your mouth for a count of six, envisioning your fears leaving your body. Imagine them dissipating into the air, replaced by the courage you just inhaled.
7. **Repeat the Process**: Continue this cycle of inhaling courage and exhaling fear for several minutes. Aim for about five to ten cycles, allowing yourself to sink deeper into relaxation with each breath.

8. **Reflect and Ground Yourself**: After completing the cycles, take a moment to sit in silence. Feel how your body feels different after this practice. Ground yourself by noticing the sensations in your body and expressing gratitude for the courage you've cultivated.
9. **Close the Practice**: When you're ready, gently open your eyes and take a moment to reorient yourself to your surroundings.

This technique can be used anytime you feel anxious or fearful. By consciously shifting your focus to courage and letting go of fear through your breath, you can create a more empowered mindset. It has truly been a transformative tool for me during some particularly challenging and confusing phases of my life and I needed a way to ground myself. I had to find a way to stay rooted in the present, no matter how difficult it was to resist the pull of the environment that had become comfortable. I knew how it made me look but I made the conscious decision to stay away from conflict while I healed. I had no interest in fighting, harboring resentment, or engaging in petty disputes with others.

As I stood at the threshold of healing, I took a deep breath of courage in filling my body with the strength and resilience that I needed to carry me through some dark moments. And I exhaled the fear, doubt, and the pain that no longer served me. I let the rhythm of my breath be a reminder that I was capable of transformation, that I could rise above the heartache and emerge stronger, wiser, and more compassionate. Inhale courage, and exhale fear became the mantra I needed to trust the process and to remind myself that I was one step closer to wholeness.

Chapter 10

A Voice

One quiet evening, after a day that had completely zapped my energy, I slipped beneath the cool sheets of my bed, yearning for rest. As I turned onto my side, a soothing calm washed over me, and I closed my eyes, surrendering to the softness of the pillow. The world outside faded into a distant hum, allowing me to drift into the threshold of sleep. In this serene moment, amidst the silence, a gentle voice broke through the stillness—a voice that was both familiar and comforting.

It was as if a warm light had broke through the chaos of my mind, cutting through the fog of distractions and worries that had plagued me throughout the day. This voice was a reminder that I was loved, that I mattered. I marveled at how, during a time so fraught with noise and uncertainty, I could still connect with the divine. I realized then that God didn't require elaborate conversations or grand gestures; sometimes, all it takes is a moment of stillness—a pause to breathe, to listen, to be open.

As I lay in that tranquil embrace, having chose to disengage from the digital world a habit that would often keep my mind racing and disconnected from the divine. No glowing screen, no frantic scrolling—just quietude. It was in this sacred space that another voice came through, a voice that filled my heart with warmth: my mother. I hadn't heard her voice in nearly two years, and the mere sound of it had an immediate calming effect. It felt like a soft embrace on a cold night.

"I can see everything here," she said, her voice imbued with love and support. She reassured me that she was watching over all of us—me, my sons, my brother, and the rest of the family. Her words spun a cocoon of safety around me, strengthening my spirit. She gently urged me not to allow the actions of those around me to rob me of my peace, reminding me that their choices were beyond my influence. I felt the weight of her wisdom, her understanding of the human experience.

She had an insightful message for me to pass on to my brother too, telling me to pass on the message that he didn't need to drown himself in alcohol to feel connected with her. She said, "Tell him I can hear him, he doesn't need to drink to talk to me," she said, her voice soft yet firm. My heart softened at her reassurance.

Then, she spoke about Ray—my husband. She acknowledged her initial doubts about our relationship but quickly corrected that notion. Her tone shifted to one of pride and acceptance as she declared, "He loves you." The relief that washed over me was palpable, with her words gifting me a sense of belonging and validation.

As she continued, she shared glimpses into our future. She described my sons with such clarity and tenderness, assuring me that Brenden, my oldest son, would find a loving wife and start a family of his own, while Dillan, my baby boy, would serve his country for twenty years. The details painted vibrant images in my mind, calming my anxieties about their paths.

In that tender moment, she spoke about a weighty decision I was wrestling with. My husband and I had been considering buying a new home, but my mother's voice resonated with clarity and certainty, advising me against it. She urged me to recall the prayers I had sent out into the universe long before I met Ray, prayers that had been heard and answered. I could almost feel the warmth of the sun on my face as she spoke of my desires, of the heartfelt entries I had penned in my journal, detailing the qualities I longed for in a partner. "God prepared Ray for you," she said, affirming that he had been ready for a loving relationship well before our paths crossed. It was as if time stood still in that moment of revelation.

Then came a heavy truth. As I had felt a lump in my breast and had an upcoming doctor's appointment, she softened the blow, saying, “I’m sorry, baby girl, it is cancer, but don’t worry; you will be okay. It’s not the end of your story; it’s just a part of the story.” Her words struck me like a bolt of lightning, both poignant and illuminating. When I received the official diagnosis, I wasn’t shocked or devastated; I had felt prepared in a way.

Waking from that profound experience, tears cascaded down my cheeks. My husband lay beside me, eyes wide as he took in the emotions swirling within me. I shared every detail with him, recounting the comfort of my mother’s voice that had soothed my soul. He was taken aback yet filled with joy for the connection I had reestablished with her.

The encounter felt impossibly real. It transcended mere dreaming. I was cloaked in darkness, but rather than fear or confusion, I was met with the brilliant clarity of my mother’s voice. Each word resonated deeply within me, carrying with it a treasure trove of love, wisdom, and hope, reminding me that even in silence, we may find the most profound truths.

It was an incredibly reassuring experience, a gentle embrace during a time when there was so much chaos, allowing clarity to seep in. Now more than ever. I have finally grasped the profound truth that I must trust in the process of life itself. I've come to understand that God desired for me to find peace with my past, was a prerequisite for propelling me toward my future, the future he envisions for me. In her unique heartfelt way, God sent my mother to come and remind me of the importance of surrendering my expectations, encouraging me to immerse gratitude in every thought, to transform even the mundane into a source of joy and appreciation. This shift in perspective was a gift that allowed me to see the beauty in my current situation, no matter how challenging.

In moments of reflection, feeling my mother's comforting presence, a divine messenger assuring me that I would never be placed in a storm that I wasn't capable of weathering. And understanding that God wasn't intent on breaking me; instead, He was guiding me toward freedom. He wanted me to navigate life's uncertainties with courage and resilience.

Overtime I gradually began to see the truth and the battles I thought would destroy me transformed into a roadmap for self-discovery. Each step through that dark valley was arduous, yet I made it through just as my mother had assured me. I allowed myself to fully absorb and appreciate every segment of my journey.

For most of my life, I had masked the pain, pretending that nothing significant had impacted my life, desperately trying to outpace the storm raging within me. But now, instead of fleeing, I stand firm, embracing my reality. The loss of my childhood innocence weighing heavily on my heart, compounded by the absence of my father throughout my life. Enduring criticism for being sensitive and emotional long before I understood my own personality traits. I allowed myself to act out of character, suppressing essentials parts of myself, all in an effort to avoid appearing weak.

While facing deep losses: my daughter, the disillusionment of divorce, and shattering of the family I had been so excited to build. The pain didn't stop there; just as I begin to believe the worst had passed, I lost my mother, a heartbreaking farewell, and friendships I believed would last a lifetime withered away. Yet, rather than hiding from these experiences, I now embrace them. I hold them close with new found confidence.

I wasn't meant to simply endure; this journey was a path toward learning, growth, and ultimately evolving into the person I was always meant to be. Each moment spent in the storm has become a vital chapter in my story, shaping who I am and guiding me toward a future that is vibrant and full of hope. The scars I carry will always be there to tell tales of resilience, and I now see the light that shines ahead, illuminating the potential for new beginnings and stronger connections.

Chapter 11

You Can

One day a close friend sent me a text illustrating a timeline of my struggles, in my opinion not in a loving supportive way, with a message “We can change actions but we are who we are. I pray your lump is stress.” which ultimately turned out to be breast cancer. Now, at first it felt like extra weight on my spirit. I wrestled with those words, feeling cornered by an identity that seemed inescapable. But, after talking with my therapist, I learned to view that time line with fresh eyes. It became a map of progress that showcased not only my endurance but also my growth.

We have already established that the desire to be chosen, to fit into predefined molds, often clouds our judgement and hampers out true potential. So, it’s no surprise that letting go of that need for external validation felt like a monumental task. Not to mention how easy it is to accept the things that stagnate you, because that requires no effort. The powerful truth is that I can seek what I deserve. I can choose to articulate my needs, voice my dissent, and pursue a life that resonates with my authentic self. It began with the realization that I don’t need to walk on eggshells to make others feel at ease. Instead, I can assert my own desires, wholeheartedly believing that I am worthy of better.

True empowerment comes from cultivating a genuine and honorable relationship with yourself. It demanded dedication and honesty—and a commitment to understanding who I am and what I want out of life. It will take time to mend and heal the parts of myself that have been bruised by past experiences and the expectations of others but I believe I can change. Through the healing process, you can reclaim your power and find the strength to rebuild your existence. It requires consistency, effort, and a vision that aligns with your core beliefs. The act of rebuilding yourself from the ground up may feel daunting, but it is also invigorating. It's an opportunity to manifest your aspirations into reality, to take ownership of your narrative.

It is not just about individual achievements; it encompasses the broader experience of reconnecting with yourself and the world around you. It involves creating a home—a safe harbor within yourself where you can find solace and strength. It's about nurturing relationships that honor your true self and infusing your life with meaning and connection.

While the road to self-empowerment is paved with challenges and setbacks, it is undeniably rewarding. From unlearning past behaviors to embracing new ones.

Acknowledging that growth is a gradual process opening the door to patience and grace as you navigate the highs and lows. Remember, no matter what anyone says you can reshape your reality, reclaim your narrative, and embrace life on your own terms. You just have to believe in your power, take ownership of your voice, and boldly step into the life you desire.

I can attest that once you choose to journey beyond the pain and you find yourself gazing into the mirror, you'll finally see a version of yourself that embodies strength and wisdom. The face looking back will reflect not just the scars of past battles but also the lessons learned through them. You'll recognize that change is not a distant hope; it is your reality. You'll have embraced transformation and, in doing so, you will have carved a path for others to follow. As you breathe in this newfound strength, remember that you are an agent of change not only for yourself but also for those around you. Embrace it fully, there's a beautiful, unique story waiting to unfold.

Part Four: The Individuality

"To be nobody but yourself in a world that's doing its best to make you somebody else, is to fight the hardest battle you are ever going to fight. Never stop fighting."

– E.E. Cummings

Chapter 12

Doubt

Doubt is a fleeting, often unsettling emotion that lingers in the back of one's mind, casting shadows over decisions and beliefs. Throughout my life, I've found myself trapped in a cycle of self-doubt, often wondering if my feelings and actions were truly my own or merely reactions to the expectations of others. I remember those moments when I felt that pressure to conform, to blend in seamlessly with the wishes of those around me. It was as if I was stuck in this unspoken agreement where I prioritized the relationships I had, fearing loneliness above all, over my own sense of self-worth.

There were times when I allowed others to dictate how I should be treated, how I should think, simply so I wouldn't risk losing their companionship. The fear of isolation was all-consuming, leading me to compromise my own greatness and worth. I became a passive participant in my own life, navigating through situations like a leaf on a river, simply going with the flow to keep the peace. This tendency, it seems, inadvertently communicated to those around me that I lacked the strength to assert my own desires and needs.

But this realization stirred something within me, a question that was hard to ignore: Did these people truly care for me and my well-being? As I began to recognize the importance of my own autonomy and started making choices that reflected my authentic self, I encountered unexpected scrutiny. Decisions that I believed were right for me were met with judgement, reflecting the discomfort of those whose expectations I had failed to meet. It became clear that my choices, when not aligned with their desires, were often deemed rash or thoughtless, revealing a deeper truth about the nature of those relationships. In striving to assert my own path, I found that some were quick to criticize rather than support, exposing the fragility of connections predicated on conformity rather than mutual respect. The moment I chose to embrace my individuality, I began to understand the complex dynamics of care and control that had shaped my interactions.

For me, doubt manifested as a nagging uncertainty, a whisper that questioned the validity of my thoughts and actions. It felt like a clenching sensation in my stomach, as if there was an invisible weight pushing down on my confidence. Through therapy I learned to use doubt in an effective way. When used in a way to honor myself that doubt led to introspection prompting me to analyze motives, evidence, and opinions. See doubt can be either enlightening or paralyzing; it can cause indecision and anxiety or it can foster critical thinking and growth. But, know that doubt is not purely negative I encourage you to try using it as a catalyst for change, pushing you to seek clarity, reconsider your path and strengthen your convictions.

With each small decision, I learned a bit more about myself. There were times that I faltered, choosing comfort over authenticity, only to be left with a nagging sense of regret. But there were also moments of clarity and I learned that I need to practice discernment. Having discernment is crucial in many aspects of life. It allows us to make informed decisions by critically evaluating information, situations, and people before forming conclusions or taking action. Discernment involves a combination of intuition and critical thinking. It helps us distinguish between what is truly beneficial or harmful and enables us to prioritize our values and principles.

In relationships, for example, discernment aids in recognizing trustworthy individuals versus those who may not have our best interest at heart. In professional setting, it helps when deciding which opportunities are worth pursuing and which risks to avoid. Essentially, having discernment empowers us to navigate life more effectively, leading to wiser choices and healthier outcomes.

In a world overflowing with information and diverse perspectives, honing our discernment can prevent us from being swayed by manipulation, misinformation, or peer pressure. It encourages us to seek deeper understanding and foster a more thoughtful approach to our interactions and decisions. Thus, cultivating discernment is not just an asset; it is another vital skill for personal growth and success.

Together doubt and discernment create a delicate balance. Where doubt prompts inquiry and reflection, discernment provides the insight needed to navigate through the complexities of life. By honoring both, we cultivate a path toward more thoughtful and intentional living, allowing us to embrace the unknown with confidence and curiosity. Having trust in yourself is a vital aspect of personal growth and well-being. It involves believing in your abilities, judgement, and values, and it plays a crucial role in how you approach challenges and opportunities in life.

I'd like to share somethings that I learned in therapy and somethings I learned while I was in the thick of my research phase:

1. **Self-Awareness**: Understanding your strengths and weaknesses is the first step. Being aware of what you

excel at and where you need improvement helps build a realistic foundation for self-trust. Reflect on past experiences and learn from them to gain insight into your capabilities.

2. **Positive Affirmations**: Engaging in positive self-talk can reinforce your self-belief. Repeating affirmations can help counteract negative thoughts and instill a sense of worthiness. Simple statements like "I am capable," or "I can handle this," can boost your confidence.

3. **Setting Goals**: Establishing achievable goals helps you to build trust in your abilities over time. Start with small, manageable objectives and gradually challenge yourself with larger ones. Each achievement reinforces your belief in yourself.

4. **Facing Fear**: Trusting yourself often means stepping out of your comfort zone. Facing fears and taking calculated risks can lead to personal growth, proving to yourself that you can handle challenges.

5. **Learning from Mistakes**: Instead of viewing failures as setbacks, consider them opportunities for learning and growth. Analyzing what went wrong and how you can improve helps to build resilience and reinforces your belief in your ability to overcome difficulties.

6. **Seeking Feedback**: While self-trust is about internal validation, seeking constructive feedback from others can provide additional perspectives. It can help you see your strengths that you may overlook and guide you on areas of improvement.

7. **Mindfulness and Self-Reflection**: Practicing mindfulness can enhance your awareness and appreciation of yourself. Regularly reflecting on your experiences, decisions, and feelings fosters a deeper connection to your inner self.

8. **Surrounding Yourself with Support**: Build a supportive network of friends, family, and mentors who encourage and uplift you. Their belief in you can help strengthen your own self-trust.

Incorporating these practices into your daily life can significantly enhance your confidence and belief in yourself, ultimately leading to a more fulfilling and empowered existence.

Chapter 13

Criticism

Throughout my life, I've encountered instances where individuals I considered "friends" have attempted to humiliate me publicly, judge me harshly, and criticize my choices in ways that felt deeply unjust. These experiences have prompted a whirlwind of questions in my mind. I often found myself wondering why these people, who professed to love and care for me, would resort to such hurtful tactics. It left me feeling confused and betrayed, as their actions contradicted their words.

A significant challenge for me during these moments was my overwhelming aversion to confrontation. I often shied away from difficult conversations, fearing that things would escalate into open conflict. As a result, I would let peoples' cutting remarks and passive-aggressive behavior linger in the air, unaddressed. Instead of confronting the hurtful shade they cast in my direction, I internalized my pain and fell into a cycle of self-doubt and frustration. I felt trapped in an emotional labyrinth, unable to find a way out because I was too afraid to seek clarity or defend myself. I didn't want to lose my friends or the glimmer of love I received from them from time to time.

Looking back, I can see that I often bore the weight of this problem on my own. By avoiding confrontation, I allowed the toxic dynamics in these friendships to fester. I realize now that by not speaking up when I needed to, I missed opportunities to establish boundaries and articulate my feelings. It's a painful yet valuable lesson about the necessity of open communication and the importance of standing firm for myself. I wish I had harnessed the courage to address these issues head-on, as it may have led to greater understanding, respect, and healthier relationships in my life.

There were times when I considered their comments to be well-intentioned or merely constructive advice. I wanted to believe that I needed their guidance more than their support and understanding. However, through these experiences, I've come to recognize that the dynamics of giving and receiving criticism, advice, and opinions - or passing judgement - are incredibly complex and sensitive matters. Understanding this has allowed me to reevaluate how I'd want to show up in people's lives as well as what I truly need from my relationships and how to set healthier boundaries moving forward.

The dangers of criticism during tough times can manifest in various ways, often compounding the already heavy burdens someone may be facing. When people are struggling, whether due to personal struggles, financial hardships, or broader societal issues harsh judgement or negative feedback can be damaging.

In moments of vulnerability, individuals may seek support and understanding, but instead encounter unwelcomed advice and criticism that further erodes their self-esteem and resilience. This kind of negative reinforcement can lead to a sense of isolation, making a person feel misunderstood or judged rather than supported.

Moreover, unwanted advice and criticism can stifle open communication, causing individuals to withdrawal and hide their challenges rather than seek help. Constant scrutiny during tough times can overshadow the genuine efforts people make to cope and adapt. Instead of acknowledging resilience or small victories, focusing solely on failures can perpetuate a cycle of hopelessness and despair. So, it's crucial to approach those facing difficulties with compassion and empathy, fostering a supportive atmosphere that encourages dialogue and healing rather than judgement. By doing so, we can help each other navigate challenges more effectively, leading to a more constructive outcome in the long run.

Criticism can be categorized into several different types, each serving a unique purpose and varying in its approach and intention. I want to share a detailed breakdown of two of the most common types of criticism:

1. **Constructive Criticism**: This type focuses on providing positive feedback alongside areas for improvement. It's aimed at helping the recipient grow and develop rather than simply pointing out flaws.

2. **Destructive Criticism**: In contrast to constructive criticism, destructive criticism often aims to belittle or demoralize the recipient. It lacks helpful suggestions and can be harmful, as it may discourage a person from trying again.

Criticism, when delivered thoughtfully, can serve as a powerful tool in nurturing relationships, be they platonic, romantic, or familial. In friendships constructive feedback can help friends understand each other's perspectives, deepening their bond. In romantic partnerships, sharing concerns can spark meaningful conversations that lead to greater intimacy and trust. Likewise, within families, open dialogue about expectations and feelings fosters a supportive environment where each member feels valued and heard.

I can't stress enough how essential it is to approach criticism with care. The key lies in balancing honesty with empathy, ensuring that the message is clear while also considering the feelings of the other person. When done right, criticism can pave the way for stronger connections and a deeper understanding of one another allowing relationships to flourish and evolve. By embracing this aspect of communication, we can build healthier dynamics that stand the test of time.

Receiving criticism and appreciating feedback are two very important skills, these are skills I've only recently started to improve, and they've had a significant impact on my growth. I had to develop a more thoughtful approach by fundamentally shifting my perspective on feedback. Recognizing that constructive criticism is not an attack but rather an invitation to improve. I had to learn to separate criticism from my self-worth, which allowed me to absorb feedback without it feeling like a personal attack.

I am learning to be a more active listener, taking into consideration the person giving the feedback. I consider their expertise or personal experience regarding the topic. For instance, my therapist is someone I know who is sharing insight with the intention of helping me grow. My biggest lesson learned is to refrain from immediate responses, learning to resist the urge to respond right away. Instead, I try to listen intently, letting the words wash over me. This process ensures that I fully grasp her perspective and the context behind their advice or criticism. I believe that by gradually adopting new practices, I can change the way I perceive and respond to criticism.

No matter how similar someone's story is to yours, it's important to recognize that even if the experiences seem identical, the emotional responses can vary greatly. Each person carries their own unique perspective, past experiences, and emotional filters that shape how they react to similar events. It's all too easy to assume you know what someone should do or how they should feel when they encounter a challenging situation, but that assumption often overlooks the depth of their emotional journey.

When you haven't faced the exact circumstances yourself, it's tempting to speak from a place of distance, proposing what you would or wouldn't do. However, even those who have gone through comparable experiences may find themselves responding in unexpected ways. What feels like a logical reaction in theory can quickly become muddled in the complexity of real emotions and personal history.

So, it's essential to approach others' experiences with empathy and an open heart, understanding that each person's emotional landscape is complex and unique. Embracing this idea can foster more profound compassion and connection, reminding us that while our stories may overlap, the emotional nuances are distinctly our own.

The phrase "none of us sit high enough to look down on anyone" conveys a powerful message about humility and equality. It suggests that, regardless of our achievements, status, or position in life, we are all fundamentally equal. This expression encourages us to recognize that everyone has their struggles and experiences, and no one is inherently superior to another.

In a world where comparisons often lead to feelings of superiority or inferiority, this perspective serves as a reminder to treat others with respect and kindness. It fosters a sense of community and belonging, highlighting the importance of understanding and empathy in our interactions with one another. By adopting this mindset, we create a more inclusive and compassionate environment, where everyone feels valued and heard.

Chapter 14

Persistence

I've come to realize that persistence is perhaps the most challenging aspect of personal development. Being human means dealing with self-doubt and fear, which can easily creep into our minds. It's a constant battle to keep those negative thoughts at bay while striving to remain productive. There have been many moments when I stumbled, feeling defeated, only to remind myself that it's okay to fall. The important part is standing back up, brushing myself off, and beginning again, and I'll be the first to admit that it's not as easy as it sounds.

For instance, while writing this book, I set a deadline and even shared it on social media to hold myself accountable. However, life has a way of intervening, and I found myself overwhelmed. My first draft turned out to be extremely rough, filled with insecurities and unrealistic expectations. Initially, I felt defeated, yet I realized that completing this project was something I truly desired. So, I decided to wipe the slate clean and start anew.

This time, I took a step back to contemplate what I truly wanted to convey and how best to express those ideas. I created a detailed outline, keeping many of the specifics to myself for focus and clarity. This journey is not just about completing a book; it's a testament to going beyond the pain and stepping into my own power.

This is where I choose to honor my heart, celebrate my worth, and embrace my unique magic. I've recognized that this isn't the time to play it small or shy away from acknowledging my greatness. Instead, it's about leaning into my ambitions and pouring all my energy into this endeavor. I refuse to give into doubts or fears any longer. This moment is about empowerment, resilience, and unwavering commitment to pursuing my dreams. It's about realizing that the only limits are those I place on myself, and I'm determined to break free from them.

Persistence in personal development can often be filled with twist and turns that can lead to frustration and self-doubt. There are several factors that contribute to the difficulty of maintaining consistency on this journey of self-improvement.

One of the primary challenges is the slow pace at which personal growth often unfolds. Unlike goals that yield immediate results, such as those in our professional or social lives, personal development requires a long-term commitment. Whether it's developing a new skill, fostering a new habit, or improving emotional well-being, these endeavors typically take time and sustained effort. The journey towards self-improvement can feel tedious, especially when the fruits of one's labor remain elusive in the early stages. This absence of immediate results can be disheartening and may lead individuals to questions whether their efforts are worthwhile.

External distractions significantly hinder an individual's ability to remain focused on their personal development goals. In today's fast-paced world, many individuals juggle multiple responsibilities-work commitments, family obligations, social engagements, and various forms of entertainment. When life becomes chaotic, self-improvement often takes a backseat. The pressing demands of daily life can create a sense of urgency that overshadows personal aspirations, leading to the neglect of growth-oriented activities. This diversion can make it difficult for individuals to crave out dedicated time for reflection, learning, and practice.

Compounding this issue is the emotional and psychological landscape that many encounter on their personal development journey. Self-doubt and fear of failure can be crippling. For many, the belief that they are not capable of achieving their developmental goals becomes a persistent mental barrier. This fear can manifest as anxiety or procrastination, causing individuals to shy away from challenges, and hindering their ability to embrace growth opportunities. When faced with obstacles, the inner critic often takes center stage, whispering thoughts of inadequacy that can lead us to retreat into our comfort zones.

Additionally, the process of personal development often requires individuals to comfort uncomfortable truths about their behaviors, beliefs, and emotional patterns. Facing these aspects of oneself can evoke a range of difficult emotions-guilt, shame, or even sadness. Such feelings can create significant resistance to change, prompting individuals to cling to old habits rather than engaging in the uncomfortable work of transformation.

Another complicating factor is the absence of a clear plan or realistic expectations. Without a well-defined roadmap, I felt overwhelmed by the enormity of my aspirations. Vague goals lead to confusion and frustration, making it challenging to measure progress and stay motivated. When milestones are not established, I struggle to recognize even small achievements, which made it easy to succumb to feelings of defeat when faced with setbacks.

The path of personal development is multifaceted and

fraught with emotional, psychological, and practical challenges. Recognizing the complexity of these obstacles was an important first step in navigating them effectively. By understanding the interplay of immediate distractions, emotional hurdles, and the need for structured goal-setting, I was able to cultivate a more persistent and patient approach to my self-improvement journey. Developing resilience, fostering self-compassion, and creating supportive environment can ultimately make the pursuit of personal growth a more achievable and rewarding endeavor.

Even the most accomplished individuals, those who have reached the heights of success, often find themselves hassling with the ongoing struggle to maintain persistence. The pursuit of their goals isn't a straight line; rather, it resembles a winding road filled with unexpected challenges and hurdles that test their resolve. Each setback can feel like a significant blow, forcing them to confront doubts and insecurities that can creep in during difficult phases.

Successful people understand that the journey demands not only talent and hard work but also an unwavering commitment to pushing forward, especially when motivation begins to wane and immediate rewards seem almost out of reach. They develop a strong sense of resilience, actively seeking ways to overcome obstacles instead of succumbing to frustration and despair.

This perseverance manifests in various ways: whether through seeking mentorship, refining their strategies, or simply taking a moment to reflect on past achievements to reignite their passion. They lean on their experiences, drawing strength from previous challenges they have overcome, which serve as reminders that persistence can ultimately lead to success.

This daily battle against the temptation to give up reveals a fundamental truth about the nature of achievement. It illustrates that behind every triumph, no matter how celebrated, lies a personal narrative filled with struggles, determination, and a relentless spirit that refuses to back down.

Chapter 15

Self-Discovery

This chapter is a deep reflection on my journey to self-discovery, sparked by a comment someone once made to me: "I'm not saying that I know you better than you know yourself, but…" from there, they launched into a monologue that felt oddly invasive, yet strangely enlightening. This moment made me realize how much I had internalized the perceptions of others, often at the expense of my own identity.

Writing this chapter is my way of reclaiming my narrative. It is exploration of my thoughts and feelings, and through this process, I hope to bridge the gap between how others perceive me and my understanding of self. I have grown since putting pen to paper, evolving beyond the version of myself I knew then. I recognize why someone might have thought they knew me better: I often lacked the confidence to assert my own opinions and allowed external influences; be it comments, judgements, or expectations, to overshadow my beliefs and values.

At my core, I identify as an empath. I often feel things deeply, wearing my heart on my sleeve. I am sensitive, intuitive, and compassionate, but this also means I struggle to remain grounded and establish healthy boundaries. The harsh realities of life can sometimes send me spiraling, leaving me anxious and overwhelmed. I am artistic and art serves as my refuge, providing a sanctuary where I can escape the chaos of knotty emotions and find comfort.

Vulnerability is a significant challenge for me, especially in emotionally unsafe environments. This extends to conflict resolution and having difficult but necessary conversations. If I do not feel emotionally secure, I struggle to communicate my wants, needs, and boundaries, frequently sacrificing my own needs for the sake of others. I now realize that this behavior disrupted my inner peace and prevented me from asserting myself in the same way I honored the needs of those around me.

My emotional ties run deep, making it extremely hard for me to detach from people I care about. If I ever decide to let someone go, know that it wasn't a decision made lightly; it required immense introspection and effort on my part. I tend to overlook flaws and can accept people for who they are, sometimes to my own detriment. My emotions heavily influence my decision-making, which has contributed to worsening situations during difficult times. For years, I allowed myself to be mishandled, demonstrating a weak will that led me to avoid confrontation. This behavior only compounded my struggles, preventing me from standing tall in my truth. Now, I'm committed to evolving, understanding my worth, and setting boundaries that honor both myself and those I care about.

I have always been someone who endures a lot of mistreatments, often to the point where it becomes overwhelming. However, everyone has a breaking point, and mine is no exception. When I finally hit that limit, I tend to shut down and distance myself. It's a protective mechanism that I've developed over time. Just because I have a tender, emotional side doesn't mean I'm foolish or that I deserve to be manipulated or taken for granted.

While I haven't shared specific names or many detailed accounts of the painful moments I've experienced, I believe that's not where the essence of my truth lies. My truth is about something deeper, it revolves around the idea of taking each experience, whether positive, negative, or neutral, and using it as a catalyst for personal growth. I strive to process these experiences in a healthy manner so that I can move forward in life, rather than getting trapped in cycles of negativity or toxicity. Through this journey, I'm learning to acknowledge my feelings and reactions, and to harness them for my evolution instead of letting them dictate my emotional state.

I used to have a strong aversion to my sensitivity. It felt like a significant weakness, a flaw that made me question my strength and resilience. But now, I've come to embrace this aspect of myself. I'm no longer running from the truth; in fact, I welcome it. I've decided to be honest and vulnerable, shedding the layers of pretense and superficiality that once held me back. I'm ready to present my authentic self to the world, without any sugarcoating.

For years, I dishonored myself by prioritizing the expectations of others over my own needs and well-being. I took out loans (up to 10K) at any given time to travel and participate in events simply to avoid disappointing those I cared about, placing their happiness above my own stability. I would drive for hours to celebrate others, pouring my time and resources into these experiences. I drove those same distances seeking recognition and celebrating for myself, though it often felt fleeting.

Over the course of four years, I embarked on twenty-one trips, some were spontaneous road trips, while others took me across borders. While I had fond memories from these travels, I didn't allow myself the space to recover from the financial strain that came with them. This journey has been a wake-up call, highlighting how I often bore the weight of these obligations alone while longing for validation and support. Often times finding myself lost in the expectations and desires of others, abandoning my own needs and wants in the process.

There were so many times, I sought approval form those around me, believing that their acknowledgement would somehow define my place in the world. This need for external validation created a cycle where I constantly measured my worth against the opinions and choices of others, thinking that my value was contingent upon their acceptance of me. I now realize that true worthiness stems from within. It's about making the choice to love and accept myself, rather than waiting for someone else to affirm my existence. I've come to understand that the blessings I've received from God were often squandered in my relentless pursuit to meet everyone else's needs. Let me be clear, I didn't feel coerced into this role; instead, it was a misguided intention stemming from a desire to nurture and love those around me.

While reflecting on my past, I noticed that there was always that little girl inside of me who equated love with fulling the needs of others. I thought that by giving thoseI loved what they craved, I was somehow making them feel loved and validated. But this perspective blinded me to my own self-worth. Now, as I embrace self-acceptance, I understand that love does not required sacrifice at the expense of my happiness. It's about balance, and it starts with valuing myself first.

I have come to define my maturity by my ability to respond to hurt with understanding rather than retaliation. When someone wrongs me, I am reminded how unsatisfied I was when I would react with anger or pain. Now, I pay attention to the complexities of their situation and I chose not to reciprocate harm. This mind set has helped me to foster healing, and allowed me to break free from a cycle where my nervous system would cling to familiar emotional turmoil and instead, I now embrace the potential for positive change.

I am learning to making different choices in response to adversity. This process of healing hasn't been straight-forward it's been a winding path filled with ups and downs. I believe that misconceptions surrounding various feelings have clouded my understanding of situations and actions.

My silence didn't guarantee me peace, and that's why I am working so hard to practice discernment and grace. I don't find drama exciting and I don't want my loyalty to be invoked by fear of losing relationships and connections. I've come to realize that toxicity cannot coexist with love; the two simply don't add up. I've learned that it is vital for the people in my life to respect my boundaries, just as I respect theirs, and if someone reacts negatively towards my boundaries it is usually an indication that there may be a lack of respect and I should take the time to decide how to address it and if necessary to step back from the relationship.

I'm now accepting the fact that I am not personally responsible for managing other people's happiness, nor am I always the root cause of their reactions to my expressed feelings, needs, decisions, or opinions. Ultimately, I cannot control others' actions or emotions, but I can control my own responses and the boundaries I set for myself.

"Emotional maturity refers to the ability to understand, manage, and express one's emotions in a healthy and constructive way. It encompasses a combination of emotional intelligence, self-regulation, empathy, and social skills, which contribute to one's overall psychological development and interpersonal effectiveness. Developing

emotional maturity is an ongoing process that requires self-reflection, practice, and a commitment to personal growth. It can significantly enhance a person's quality of life, improve relationships, and contribute to overall well-being."

It took me quite some time to fully grasp the idea that my reactions often have little impact on the world around me and no amount of my emotional responses will magically evoke love or respect from others. I can't force someone to appreciate me or alter their perceptions simply through my fervent responses.

I've found that some situations are better left as they are. Fighting for closure or relentlessly seeking explanations can be draining and pointless. Chasing after answers or trying to make people understand my perspective has led me to being frustrated. What I've slowly learned is that I'm better off redirecting my focus inward, rather than allowing external circumstances to dictate my happiness or sense of self-worth.

By centering my life on my thoughts and feelings, rather than what others think or do, I am embracing a more fulfilling way of being. This shift in perspective has taught me that true peace comes from within, and it's okay to let go of when necessary. Life became significantly enriched when I nurtured my inner world.

In my pursuit of becoming a Licensed Mental Health Counselor, my vision extends far beyond merely fixing problems or offering unsolicited advice. I am aware that each individual's journey is uniquely their own, filled with struggles and triumphs that I may never fully comprehend. It's essential to me that I don't project my assumptions onto others, believing I know more about their lives than they do. Instead, I aspire to create a safe space where people feel heard and validated, where they can explore their own thoughts and emotions without the weight of judgement.

My intention is to remind individuals that they are not broken, and that their experiences, no matter how challenging, are part of their valuable human story. By actively listening and providing a compassionate ear, I aim to help them uncover their own wisdom and insights. I want to give them the chance to articulate their feelings and thoughts, guiding them gently towards the realization that they possess the expertise required to navigate their own lives.

I don't hold all the answers, no one does. As a Mental Health Counselor my role will be to support, to offer companionship on my future client's path to self-discovery, and to help them learn how to sit with the difficulties of life instead of running from them. I'm inspired by those who have helped me on my journey, and my hope is to pay that kindness forward helping others find their strength and resilience in the face of their own adversities.

Chapter 16

Ask God; Trust God

God's purpose for your life can often feel unique and distinct, especially when it diverges from the expectations of society. The world tends to measure success and purpose through conventional standards, such as wealth, status, and societal approval. However, the calling you receive from God may not always align with these metrics, and that's perfectly okay. I don't say this without the understanding that we all have financial responsibilities among other things so we handle our priorities until there's room to take action to make our dreams a reality.

In moments when you feel misunderstood or questioned by those around you, it's vital to root yourself in faith. Confidence in God's plan for you is crucial, even amid confusion and doubt. This means believing that your path has been laid out for you with divine intention, regardless of weather others can see or appreciate it.

Your journey will require courage and resilience. There may be times when you feel isolated in your convictions or purpose, but it's those very moments that call for a deeper connect when it comes to your relationship with God. By trusting in His ability to work through you, you can navigate challenges and stay true to your calling, even if it defies common logic or societal norms.

Engaging with a supportive community and seeking guidance through prayer and reflection can strengthen your resolve, helping you to embrace and fulfill your God-given purpose unapologetically. Stand firm in your faith, and take steps forward with the assurance that you are fulling a unique role in the larger gamut of life.

Self -discovery can be a transformative journey, and for me, it culminated in a moment of weighty introspection and urgency. I found myself standing at a metaphorical crossroads, each path shrouded in fog and uncertainty. The weight of these life-changing decisions pressed heavily on my heart, stirring a whirlwind of confusion and fear within me. With my mind racing and my heart pounding, I turned to God, seeking comfort and understanding in the midst of it all. Faith, whether in ourselves, others, or a higher power, demands vulnerability. But, trusting God, means trusting in something that isn't always visible but guaranteed to show up according to God's timing. This leap of faith can be daunting because it involves relinquishing control and accepting that no particular outcome is definite.

In that scared space of prayer, I poured out my feelings, confessing my doubts and vulnerabilities. The concept of an all-seeing God implies a divine presence that is aware of everything, including our innermost thoughts and intentions. But, to truly embrace this relationship, I needed to demonstrate strength by admitting my flaws, shortcomings, and mistakes. This act of vulnerability is not a sign of weakness but rather a courageous step towards personal honesty and growth. By recognizing my imperfections, I was able to open myself up to the possibility of transformation and healing. While God does see all, my journey required me to actively engage in the process of self-discovery, by demonstrating my commitment to growth and my desire to become a better version of myself.

Surrendering control was a steep and rocky road. The practice of relaxing into that trust was challenging; I often found my thoughts racing back to doubt, holding onto the need for certainty. I had to remain determined to quieting the noise in my mind, to still the restless tides of anxiety that threatened to overwhelm me. I desperately wanted to learn how to listen to His voice patiently waiting for signs, signals, and the gentle nudges that guided my heart.

Moments of stillness became my sanctuary. I began to embrace the beauty of silence, aligning my spirit with His purpose. I spent time in prayer and reflection, observing the world around me, hoping to garner insights from the daily life unfolding in front of me. It was a delicate dance of faith, where each step required courage to lean deeper into trust. God's presence became my compass, steering me through the storm of emotions and guiding me toward clarity. This experience taught me the value of deep-seated faith, reminding me that sometimes, in order to find ourselves, we must first let go and listen. I'll admit that this process can bring up insecurities and past traumas, making it a complex and sometimes painful experience. However, it's through facing these fears that we often find our greatest strengths and insights.

And when God does finally reveal something profound or personal to you, remember it's not always meant for you to share openly with friends or family. This revelation can be deeply personal and often requires contemplation and discernment. The understanding or insight might be intended to help you grow spiritually or prepare you for future challenges rather than to be broadcasted to the world. Navigating social media can be overwhelming, particularly during challenging periods in life. It's easy to get caught up in the constant flow of information and the expectations that come with having an online presence. After engaging with it for an extended time, I've reached points where a break felt necessary. Most recently it's been approximately seven months, and during this period, I've realized just how much I needed to step back from that online environment. Taking time away has allowed me to reflect, recharge, and focus on my well-being without the distractions and pressures that social media often brings. It's important to recognize when it's time to disconnect and prioritize mental health.

In today's social media age, there's tendency to share every thought or revelation, but some truths may need to be held close to our hearts. They can serve as a guide or comfort in our personal journey, and sharing them prematurely might lead to misunderstanding or unnecessary pressure. It's important to reflect on these moments and seek wisdom on weather they should be shared with others, at all. Sometimes, silence can be just as powerful as speaking out.

During my struggles, my unwavering faith in God became a powerful source of strength and hope. I stayed away from social media and confidently leaned on my family, who provided steadfast support and unconditional love. My friends stood by me, bringing laughter, light, and space when needed even in my darkest moments. With the invaluable guidance of my Christian therapist, I skillfully navigated my emotions and faced my fears head-on. I am deeply grateful for the love, wisdom, and support surrounding me, which formed a solid foundation that empowered me to rise above challenges and embrace resilience.

To me the phrase “ask God; trust God” encapsulates a thoughtful spiritual principle centered around faith and reliance on a higher power. “Ask God” signifies the act of prayer or supplication, where individuals express their desires, concerns, and hopes to the divine. This part emphasizes the importance of communication with God, inviting believers to seek guidance, support, or clarity in their lives. It suggests an active engagement in one’s faith journey, encouraging followers to articulate their needs and aspirations.

On the other hand, “trust God” represents a deep-seated confidence in God’s plan and wisdom. It signifies letting go of anxiety and embracing faith that, regardless of the challenges faced, there is a greater purpose at play. This trust invites individuals to surrender their worries and believe that, even in uncertainty, they are being guided towards what is best for them.

Together, these phrases underscore a holistic approach

to having faith; encouraging both the act of seeking divine assistance and the peace that comes from trusting in a higher power's wisdom and timing. It's an invitation to foster a personal relationship with God that encompasses both asking for help and embracing the outcomes with faith.

Embrace your individuality, for it is the essence of who you are. Doubt may creep in, but remember that criticism often comes from those who cannot see your vision. Persistence is most important; keep pressing forward even when the road gets tough. Engage in self-discovery; explore your passions, values, and beliefs. Don't hesitate to ask God for guidance, for in moments of uncertainty, faith can illuminate your path. Trust the journey and know that each step brings you closer to your true self. Your unique journey holds the power to inspire others. Keep pushing forward and let your light shine!

Part Five: Never Give Up

"One day you will tell your story of how you overcame what you went through and it will be someone else's survival guide."

– Brene Brown

Chapter 17

Choosing Me

There comes a time in life when silence speaks louder than words, exhaustion feels heavier than any physical weight, and emotional pain becomes so familiar that it almost feels like comfort. Often, these moments arise from consistently abandoning yourself to meet the expectations, needs, and demands of others. But healing begins when you make one bold decision: To stop waiting for someone else to choose you and instead, choose yourself.

Choosing yourself is not a selfish act. It is a sacred acknowledgement that you matter. It's declaring that your voice, your emotions, and your boundaries are not just valid they are essential. I was someone who lived in the shadows of codependency, people pleasing, and emotional neglect. At first choosing myself felt wrong, but it's not wrong its restorative.

When I started choosing myself, I no longer sought approval from external sources. I stop chasing validation and begin cultivating inner peace. And that is the fertile ground where I began to truly heal mentally and emotionally. As an act of self-respect, I started to set better boundaries. I began to recognize where my energy leaked. I became aware of the relationships, conversations, habits, and environments that drained me. Most importantly I had to learn to say no:

- No to overextending.
- No to emotional manipulation.
- No to situations that dishonored my well-being.

Each boundary became an act of self-respect. It's not about shutting people out it's about creating space where I could heal. I stop existing in survival mode and started living from place of intention so that I could reconnect with my authentic self. I spent so much of my life trying to be who others wanted me to be. I lost touch with who I really was a long time ago so I had to strip away my mask of emotional numbness and rediscover the person underneath. I started to ask myself:

- What do I truly want?
- What lights me up?
- What parts of myself have I silenced to keep the peace?

The process of reconnecting with myself was not always comfortable. But it was necessary. It was only when I returned to my authentic self that my mind and emotions begin to repair the damage of years of being disconnected.

Learning to self soothe instead of suppress. So many times,

I tried to heal by avoiding pain. But I know now that the real healing comes from moving through it, not around it. Choosing myself meant learning to hold space for my emotions. Instead of silencing them with distractions, substances, or toxic positivity. Now, I listen. I validate my sadness. I honor my anger. I give my grief room to breathe. Doing this gave my nervous system a chance to relax. My mind no longer has to suppress what's screaming to be acknowledge. That's when my emotions being to heal, not because I fixed them, but because I felt them.

Now healing didn't mean I'd never feel that pain again, it just meant that the pain no longer owned me. As I continue to choose myself, my outer world begins to mirror my inner healing. I started forming relationships based on mutual respect. I woke up feeling more grounded. I stopped apologizing for who I am. I let go of the need to explain myself, I started to live honestly and that honesty became the most powerful form of freedom.

Choosing yourself isn't a single decision, it's a lifelong practice. There will be days you forget. Days you fall back into old patterns. Days when fear sounds louder than self-love. But every time you return to yourself with compassion, you are rewriting the narrative of your life. You are no longer waiting to be rescued. You are becoming your own rescue. My next step was to begin building sustainable habits that support my emotional growth. So, I started with self-awareness, not self-improvement. Before I tried to build a habit, I had to ask myself:

- What emotional needs am I trying to meet?
- Is this habit rooted in self-care, or self-criticism?
- Is this habit something I genuinely want, or something I think I "should" do?

There were to many times when I built habits out of shame or pressure, which lead to me feeling burnt out. I know now that emotional growth habits should feel kind, even if they challenge you. Emotionally supportive habits are born from love, not lack. So, I anchored my habits to my emotional values, because a habit will only be sustainable if it's deeply connected to what matters to you most.

Self-awareness is a gift. It's the ability to examine your thoughts, motives, patterns, and behaviors with honesty and insight. It leads to growth, maturity, and meaningful relationships. But like any powerful tool, when misused, it can become destructive. This happens when someone uses their understanding of their flaws, triggers, or trauma as a shield to avoid accountability or as a sword to beat themselves up. When we weaponize our self-awareness, we can often still sound emotionally intelligent. We can still be good at articulating our feelings, wounds, and patterns with great detail. But the presence of insight doesn't always mean the presence of healing. It's possible to be fully aware of your behavior and still refuse to grow from it. It's also possible to explain your actions and still repeat them without remorse. Awareness alone just isn't enough, it's what we do with that awareness that defines our character.

Self-awareness should lead to self-ownership. Going to therapy and being committed to the process helped me to understand that I don't need to be perfect to grow. Growth simple means improvement. So, if your self-awareness keeps you stuck in shame or cycles of damage, it's time to start questioning whether you're using your insight to heal or to hide. When I started to heal one of the first things, I did was gather information. Gathering information was a step I took to try to make sense of what has happened, why it affected me the way it did, and what it meant for my life moving forward.

Trauma is not just the event itself; it's also the impact the event had on you. Two people can experience similar circumstances, but only one may carry lifelong pain while the other heals more quickly. Trauma is personal and recovery is never one-size-fits-all. Before I was able to heal my body needed context. My nervous system needed to regain a sense of safety, and my heart, overwhelmed by confusion and shame, needed understanding. That's why I started gathering pieces of the puzzle—memories, emotions, patterns, and reactions. Then I started reading, going to therapy, journaling, talking to others with similar experiences, and often times simply reflecting. I Eventually started to move further away from chaos and move closer to clarity—not perfect clarity, but the beginning of understanding. I needed to identify what I needed to heal.

There is power in identifying. There is freedom in realizing, *"I'm not alone in this."* Information didn't fix everything but it gave me tools. It gave me perspective. It helped me to build a foundation for digging deeper—processing, grieving, releasing, and rebuilding. This part of my journey was very overwhelming. I discovered questions that needed answers. I even uncovered something that I long buried. But the journey wasn't about rushing to fix things, it was about sitting with the truth long enough to understand it.

I am an empath and being an empath—is both a gift and a curse. I have this ability to connect, understand, and support people with a generous amount of emotional depth. But without clear boundaries and consistent self-care, it can become emotionally exhausting and I can even lose my identity. Creating a balance between having compassion for others and caring for myself is essential to my mental health. See I don't just observe other people's emotions; I often absorb them. So being in crowded spaces, emotionally intense conversations, or even something as simple as watching the news can sometimes feel overwhelming. I have to be careful and always have ways to ground myself because constantly feeling what others feel—pain, anxiety, anger—can drain my emotional energy. There were so many times, that absorbing other people's emotions on top of feeling my own, manifested as chronic fatigue, irritability, emotional numbness, and feeling lost in the needs of others. Some of the self-care practices that were helpful for me included:

- Alone time (to decompress and process emotions)
- Grounding techniques (walking in nature)
- Creative outlets (painting, writing, or even just listen to music—I created a playlist called "loving on me")

- Saying no and honoring my limits (without guilt)
- Mindful consumption (using my "Do Not Disturb" settings, social media detoxing, and setting time limits on my social media apps)

There was a time, not that long ago, I carried fear around setting boundaries because I didn't want to come off as being cold or uncaring. I understand now that boundaries are not walls—they are filters. They protect my energy while still allowing space for connection. I had to learn to say "I care about you, but I need time for myself." That was the most powerful act of self-respect and emotional clarity that I have ever made.

Therapy taught me that boundaries also involve recognizing that someone else's emotional burden is not mine to carry. That I can offer support without absorbing the weight. That I can listen deeply without losing my center. Initially I struggled a lot with guilt when I began to put myself first. But over time I learned to embrace it and I started using the "oxygen mask on a plan" theory: you have to secure your own before helping someone else. As an empath I can't offer a healing presence, that I value so much, if I am burnt-out. Rest is replenishment for me and that doesn't make me less caring it makes me more sustainable.

To honor my strength, I must first honor myself, and understand that my needs matter just as much as everyone else's. Practicing true self-care allows me to remain open-hearted, whole and creates space for my empathy to thrive and not at the cost of my own well-being, but in harmony with it.

Choosing me also made me look at and become more aware of other habits such as overthinking and my ability to operate with discernment. As an over-thinker my mind rarely rests. I will replay conversations long after they're over, questions decisions even after they're made, and I'll try to prepare for every possible outcome—especially the worst ones. Overthinking wasn't just about me thinking a lot, it was about me thinking too much about everything—often to the point of exhaustion. Being an over-thinker meant I noticed things, I pick up on small changes in tone, body language, and words others would overlook or quickly forget. My mind would always be scanning, analyzing, and trying to make sense of things—and that was often driven by a desire to avoid regret, misunderstandings, or failure. Much like being an empath it can be a strength but without boundaries it can also be extremely harmful.

Being an over-thinker without boundaries, would leave me stuck in the decision-making because I would over-analyze every option. I worried about problems that didn't exist yet, or scenarios that may never happen. I constantly questioned past actions, words, and choices. I also suffered from severe mental fatigue, not from physical work, but from carrying a mind that I could never seem to turn off.

I believe that my overthinking is a result of my childhood trauma, where my mind learned to stay alert to protect itself. It's like my brain was working to not be surprised or hurt again. While being an over-thinker help me avoid problems it also gave me the space to create imaginary problems that felt just as real. It's like my mind was constantly building, it was building both bridges and barriers—bridges to insight and barriers to peace. I needed better tools to manage this part of myself so those same self-care tools I mention earlier (page 165-166) became useful once again. I still have a tendency to be an over-thinker but I work really hard to be mindful so that it doesn't become my master. Now I know peace is possible even for a restless mind like mine.

Operating in true discernment is a much more difficult task. Because discernment is more than intelligence, and it's deeper than instinct. Discernment is the ability to see clearly, especially when clarity isn't obvious. It's knowing how to tell the difference between what feels right and what is right. Between what is good and what is best. Between what looks spiritual and what is truly of God. In a noisy world filled with opinions, emotions, and distractions, discernment is not optional it's essential. First, what is discernment? At its core discernment is the practice of wisely perceiving truth, especially when deception or confusion is present. It's the difference between reacting and responding. Between rushing and reflecting. It helps you recognize the subtle difference between truth and half-truth; emotion and conviction; opportunity and distraction; timing and delay; God's voice and your own desire. Discernment isn't about being suspicious or overly cautious. It's about being spiritually awake and mentally grounded.

Discernment is not a form of judgement or assumption. Judgement jumps to conclusions. Discernment pauses to seek understanding. Judging assumes based on the surface. While discernment digs deeper, listens longer, and often waits before speaking. Where judgement divides, discernment protects. Where judgement condemns, discernment clarifies. Discernment is wise love in action. Discernment didn't come to me naturally it was a skill I needed to pray for and cultivate. So, during my times of self-reflection, I allow life's lessons to teach me, I allow my pain to teach me. I pay attention to the consequences of my choices and the choices of others. I prayed to God and asked him to place the gift of discernment on my heart and in my mind. I pay attention to my community and my circle so that when I seek counsel it is wise and I am patient.

Discernment is extremely important, we live in a world obsessed with image, influence, and speed. Discerement reminds us to look beyond the obvious. Just because something feels good doesn't mean it's good for you. Just because something is trending doesn't mean it's true. Just because someone uses spiritual language doesn't mean they're led by the Spirit. Discernment can help you navigate relationships, decisions, teachings, and seasons of life. It can help you decide when to act and when to wait, when to speak and when to be silent, when to fight and when to let go. Discernment requires you to stay rooted in the truth, to ask questions, practice humility, to listen more than you speak, and to pray for wisdom because discernment isn't just taught—it's revealed. Discernment is a quiet strength, it doesn't boast, instead it guards. It doesn't rush, it moves at the right time. It's the difference between stumbling in the dark and walking with the light. I promise you, in every area of life—relationships, faith, career, purpose—discernment will lead you further than charisma ever will.

Chapter 18

Hi God, it's me again

It's a simple phrase. Just six words. But within them lies the weight of honesty, vulnerability, and a quiet kind of courage. "Hi God, it's me again, "was the sound of my voice—wounded but willing, tired but trying. It was the beginning of my prayer because I didn't know what to say, but still I showed up. It was not the polished language of religion, but the raw language of relationship. There was no performance in my greeting—just presence.

The phrase carried an unspoken truth that I've come to God before. Just yesterday, just an hour ago. Countless times over the same heartbreak, the same fear, the same mistakes. And yet, I come to Him again. Because I trusted on some level—that God hasn't grown tired of me. That He still listens. That He still cares.

"Hi God, it's me again," is the spiritual equivalent of coming home after a long day. You don't knock. You don't explain. You just walk through the door because you know you're allowed to be there. It's not dramatic or profound—it's real.

God has never been impressed by outward displays of religion. Ceremonies, titles, and rituals may capture the attention of people, but they do not move the heart of God unless they are anchored in truth and humility. What God desires most is not a polished reputation, but a broken and contrite heart.

In scripture, we see this over and over again. The Pharisees, experts in religious law, wore their spiritual credentials like badges of honor. They fasted, prayed publicly, and held positions of influence—yet Jesus rebuked them harshly. Why? Because their hearts were far from God. They craved approval more than transformation. They sought to appear righteous rather than become righteous.

True repentance is different. It doesn't parade itself; it pleads for mercy. It isn't concerned with appearances; it's concerned with change. Real repentance is when a person sees the weight of their sin—not just as a violation of rules, but as a rupture in their relationship with God—and they turn, not just in sorrow, but in surrender.

God listens to the one who whispers, "Have mercy on me, a sinner." not the one who proudly says, "I thank you that I am not like other people. He draws near to the humble, to the broken, to those who don't care about their spiritual résumé but desperately want a clean heart. Religious reputation may fool others, but it never fools God. He sees past the surface, into the motives, into the soul. What pleases Him is not perfection, but honesty. Not status, but surrender.

So, I laid down my mask and pretenses. I stop managing my image and start opening my heart. Because God is not looking for people who look holy—He's looking for people who are willing to be made holy.

It wasn't that long ago everything in my life felt unsteady. My mind was running in loops of anxiety. My emotions swinging back and forth between numbness and overwhelm. I was reaching for distractions, people, routines, but nothing seemed to anchor me. In those moments what I thought I needed was more control, but what I really needed was more connection to God. I didn't need outward perfection, I needed inward peace. I didn't need a quick fix—but a quiet, sacred relationship with the One who never moves, never changes, and never leaves.

It is through that relationship—personal, consistent, and intimate—that I was able to begin to ground myself mentally and emotionally, no matter what was happening around me. When my relationship with God became my foundation, I stopped relying on unstable people or temporary things to regulate my emotions. I begin to live from the inside out—anchored in something eternal, not external.

Now, for a long time I struggled to talk to God because I thought prayer had to sound polished, holy, or religious. But grounding yourself through God begins with honesty, unfiltered conversations, not memorized prayers and perfect language. God is not waiting for a performance. He's waiting for your presence. And when you begin to talk to Him—not at Him—you create space for a two-way relationship where you can receive comfort, guidance, conviction, and peace.

Overtime this relationship became my home base, a place where I could always return to, no matter how far I drifted. The more I build my relationship with God, the more I started to recognize the voice or truth over the voice of trauma and fear. God's truth gives my mind something unshakable to stand on. Over time, I begin to think and feel differently—not because I forced change, but because I let God transform me from the inside out.

Emotional and mental grounding through God requires regular connection, not just crisis-based communication. Just like any relationship, the more time you spend together, the stronger the bond becomes. Let me give you a heads up, there will be seasons when God feels silent. Or when your emotions are so heavy, you can't sense His nearness. Don't confuse silence with absence. God's love is not based on your feelings. He is still present, and sometimes He's working most deeply when He seems most quiet.

I can't stress this enough, even if you can't hear Him right now—He is still holding you. And your personal, daily relationship with Him can become the most grounding, healing, emotionally stabilizing force in your life. Not because everything will always feel okay. But because you won't be facing any of it alone.

A prayer for grounding:

God, when my emotions overwhelm me, be my peace. When my thoughts spiral, be my clarity. When I feel unsteady, be my anchor. Teach me to talk to you with honesty. Help me listen to your voice above the noise. Draw me close every day, and build in me a life grounded in Your love.

Amen.

Chapter 19
Alignment

To be in alignment with yourself is to live in such a way that your inner world matches your outer actions. It's when your thoughts, feelings, values, and choices move in the same direction—no longer pulling you in conflicting paths or forcing you to pretend. Alignment isn't about perfection. It's about congruence. It's about feeling at peace with who you are, what you're doing, and where you're going.

When you're aligned with yourself, you stop second-guessing every move or seeking validation for every decision. You trust your intuition, not because you always know the outcome, but because you've learned to trust your own voice. You make choices not out of fear, guilt, or habit, but out of clarity and intention.

Being out of alignment felt heavy, I would say yes when I meant no., I tolerated things that hurt my spirit. I would over explain, overcompensate, and overthink because something inside of me was fighting to be excepted and loved. The more I ignored my inner voice, the louder my anxiety, frustration, and fatigue became. But the moment that I returned to myself, when I really listened, really honored what was true for me I started to feel grounded. Peace began to replace pressure, and wholeness replace hustle. I begin to move though life with more ease, because I was no longer betraying myself to fit into spaces that weren't meant for me.

Alignment is freedom. It's choosing to live in a way that doesn't fracture your soul. It's the quiet confidence of showing ups as you are, without needing to prove or pretend. Once you taste that kind of freedom, it's hard to go back. Being in alignment with yourself means that who you are on the inside is fully reflected in how you live on the outside. It means your actions, words, decisions, relationships, and priorities are rooted in your deepest truth—not fear, not approval-seeking, and not survival patterns.

When you're aligned, there's no internal tug-of-war between who you're supposed to be and who you really are. There's a sense of peace that doesn't depend on your circumstances, because it comes from living authentically and unapologetically. You're no longer shape-shifting to be accepted. You're no longer shrinking to stay safe. Alignment doesn't mean life is easy. It means you're honest. It means you're clear. It means you can lay your head down at night and feel at peace with how you're showing up in the world—even if no one understands.

I am now and I will always be a work in progress. When

I was misaligned, I was emotionally exhausted, mentally scattered, spiritually distant, and physically unwell. Misalignment builds up slowly. It starts when you say "yes" to things you don't want. When you ignore your intuition. When you abandon your boundaries. When you keep choosing comfort over growth. When survival requires you to be someone else just to stay safe or feel loved. It's time to realign with yourself so that everything can shift.

You start hearing your voice again. You trust it. You make choices that feel nourishing, not depleting. You stop betraying yourself to be liked or accepted. You stop abandoning your needs for temporary peace. Alignment is quiet, but powerful. It is not loud or flashy. You don't fall into alignment by accident—it's the daily practice of returning to yourself with open arms. For me, self-honesty was an important step toward alignment. Your body knows when something's off. Pay attention to how you feel physically when you make decisions, speak with someone, or walk into a room. Tight chest, sinking gut, heavy shoulders, your body is speaking truth—listen.

Realignment required that my boundaries reflect what I truly cared about, and I had to realize that not everyone will like my boundaries and that's okay my life doesn't need to make everyone else comfortable. I had to learn how to be still, stillness reveals what noise drowns out. Journaling, prayer, meditation, or taking a quite walk are all things that helped me to get reacquainted with myself. Even with all of the work I've done, at times I've drifted, I forgot, I even fallen out of alignment. But I had to remind myself that the goal is not perfection—it's awareness.

Choosing alignment is choosing yourself. It's not always easy. It might cost you relationships, opportunities, or approval. But it will give you peace, and peace is priceless. Being in alignment isn't about becoming someone new—it's about unbecoming everything you're not, so that what's real can finally breathe again. So, I had to give myself permission to change. To course-correct. To stop explaining. To live in a way that feels like truth. Because when your soul and your actions match, the healing is undeniable. The peace is sustainable. The life I've built is mine—not a performance, but a reflection. I knew I was in alignment when peace no longer felt like a luxury, but a lifestyle.

Chapter 20
Intentional Days

Intentionality is how I stop surviving and start living. It's how l began to move through life with clarity, purpose, and direction, rather than letting life happen to me while I remained on autopilot. To be intentional meant that I had to make conscious choices, and not emotional reactions. It meant that I had to live by my values, not my fears. Most of all it meant that I was the one who got to decided how I show up in my own life, in my relationships, and in my growth.

Our time is our most sacred currency. Every moment we give away without thought or purpose is a moment we can't get back. Being intentional with my life looked like knowing what mattered most and building my life around that. Saying yes to what aligns, no to what doesn't, and designing my days to reflect my purpose not outside pressures. I was in no rush. I wasn't in competition. I just asked myself one day "Is this the life I actually want or just the one I've become used to?"

Chile! Growth is hard. Every choice no matter how big or small can either cause momentum or delay in every area of life. Love, relationships, and my growth overall, being intentional was going to be the glue holding it all together.

Being intentional with love is very important, because love is not something that just happens. Healthy love, deep and lasting love requires intention and not just in regard to who you choose to love. When you choose to give love be you must be present not performative. You should give love from a full cup, and not to fill an empty one. Choose relationships where your love is received, not just required.

The BIG! Ahaha moment for me was when I learned that intentional love also meant first loving myself— not in a selfish way, but in a foundational one. See when I started loving myself fully and with intention, I stopped begging for crumbs and confusing intensity with loyalty. Now, I love myself with wisdom, boundaries, and freedom. I stopped asking, "Do they love me?" And I began asking myself "Does this love honor who I am?"

Because, not everyone deserves a front-row seat in my life. Not every connection is meant to be permanent. And not every relationship is healthy just because it's familiar. Be intentional about who you surrounded yourself with, Ask yourself questions like:

- "Do they bring out the best in me?"
- "Can I be myself around them?"

- “Is this relationship rooted in mutual respect—or one-sided effort?”

This doesn’t mean that my intentional relationships are perfect. But they are conscious. They involve honesty, reciprocity, and the freedom to growth without guilt. They make space for truth, not just comfort. You don’t need a lot of people. You need the right people. And that requires the courage to stop watering what’s already dead.

Healing doesn’t happen by accident. Growth doesn’t happen overnight. It takes deliberate effort to become who you are meant to be. The growth process required that I check in with myself regularly. I had to let go of who I used to be, so I can make space for who I was becoming. I had to choose discipline over distraction. Over time I began to realize that growth is comfortable but often times discomfort leads to depth. Also, there will be times when growth feels slow or invisible and, in those moments, I need to continue showing up, I need to keep choosing the version of me that refuses to live a small, safe life.

Your future self is built by today’s intentional actions. You can’t just hope you’ll grow. You have to decide to grow and build your life around that decision. Intentionality isn’t about controlling everything—it's about aligning yourself with what matters. It's how you create a life that reflects your values, not just your habits. It's how you cultivate a true and lasting love with yourself, build relationships that uplift, and open yourself up to the kind of growth that transforms you from the inside out.

Unintentional love on the other hand is performative, inconsistent, and often manipulative—whether we realize it or not. It's based on pleasing, proving, or holding on out of fear. Intentional love is *chosen*, not just felt. It's not built on emotional highs or constant validation, but on respect, presence, and a desire to truly see and serve each other. It's when you look at someone—not to complete you, but to *walk* with you. It's important to note that the kind of love starts within. You must love yourself with intention: speak to yourself with kindness, even when you're not at your best. Set boundaries that protect your metal health and emotional wellness, not to punish others.

Practice forgiveness, not just toward others, but toward the past versions of yourself that didn't know any better. You teach the world how to love you by how you love yourself. And when you move with that kind of intentional love, you stop chasing those who can't meet you there. You realize that your love is scared—and it should be handled with care.

Intentional relationships require discernment. Not everyone is meant to walk with you forever. And that's not rejection—it's redirection. When I lived without intention, I kept people around based on shared history, convenience, or guilt. I let energy-drainers stay in my life because it felt easier than having a hard conversation. I settled for surface connections because I thought to myself, "they're not that bad."

But when I became intentional, I started asking myself questions like: Does this relationship add to my peace or subtract from it? Am I being authentic here—or walking on eggshells? Are we growing together, or just staying connected out of habit? Intentional relationships have depth. They're rooted in mutual respect, emotional safety, and honesty—even when it's uncomfortable. I no longer chase people. I no longer beg to be understood. I show up as I am—and let those who are aligned meet me where I am.

Intentional growth means owning my evolution. It means I'm no longer blaming my past for my patterns—

it's taking radical responsibility for what I allow now. It also means honoring my pace, I'm not behind. I'm not too late. I am exactly where I am meant to be, I just have to keep moving forward with purpose. It doesn't matter if I'm moving slow, if anyone sees it yet, or if my growth is happening in the dark. Intentionality reminds me that I am becoming—and becoming takes time.

To live with intention takes courage—because it often means breaking away from what's comfortable. I outgrew friendships that once defined me. I had to walk away from the version of success that no longer fulfilled me. I had to set boundaries with people I once feared losing. I spoke the truth that shook the foundation of my old self, and the truth was I couldn't heal, evolve, or find peace in a life that was not aligned with who I really am. Being intentional isn't just about goals or time-blocking. It's about integrity—being whole. It's about creating a life that feels good on the inside, not one that just looks good on the outside.

Life is too scared to live on autopilot. Love is too deep to give away without thought. Relationships are too valuable to be one-sided, and your growth is too important to leave to chance. So let your life be a reflection of your intention, not your fear, not your past, not you're programming, honor:

Your intention.
Your truth, and
Your opportunity to become.

Chapter 21

That Dream

Everyone carries dreams. Some whisper quietly in the corners of our minds. Others shout with the urgency of a heart on fire. I believe dreams shape who we are and who we hope to become. But life sometimes makes us ask the hardest question, "***Is it too late to chase my dreams?***" When I was thinking about what God's purpose for my life was, I started dreaming about becoming a woman who would help others navigate life's trials and heal from past traumas. I felt this heaviness—looking at the years behind me and wondering if the chance has passed. Society, outside voices, and even my own fears whispered: "*You're too old.*" Or "*It's unrealistic now.*" But, here's the truth; it's never too late. Dreams don't expire. There is no deadline stamped on your hopes and dreams. Dreams don't come with expiration dates like milk in the fridge. They live within you as long as you do—waiting patiently for your courage to catch up. When I researched it, history is full of people who began their greatest journeys late in life:

- Grandma Moses started painting at age 78.
- Colonel Sanders franchised KFC in his 60s
- Vera Wang began her fashion career at 40.

These stories aren't exceptions—they're reminders that dreams can bloom when the timing feels right for you. Sometimes the feeling that it's too late is a mask for fear—fear of failure, fear of judgement, or fear of stepping into the unknown. Fear convinces us that the safest choice is to let our dreams go, to settle for what feels "realistic." Settling means trading your *potential* for *comfort*. And that trade often leads to regret, not peace.

My dream doesn't look the same as I once imagined, and that's okay. Dreaming is about flexibility, it's about finding new ways to pursue my passions in a way that fits my life right now. It's not the size of the dream but the depth of the pursuit. It's about showing up for myself with curiosity, courage, and persistence—even if the path looks different from what I expected. Success isn't just about reaching the destination—it's also about the courage to keep moving forward.

Time has a way of making dreams feel fragile. When I was younger, my dreams felt like stars within reach—bright, urgent, and full of possibility. But as years passed, the noise of life, responsibilities, setbacks, and self-doubt can make those dreams seem distant, dimmed, and even forgotten. I had to hold on tightly to my dreams because life's realities—financial strain, family obligations, health challenges often times required me to push them aside.

"Is it too late?" A question that often carries heavy emotions—such as fear of regret, frustration, and even sadness. While life is lifin'; it sometimes feels like a door closing slowly, and the key is slipping just a tad out of reach. But let's take note here. Because feelings, while real, don't always tell the truth. The belief that it's too late is often a self-imposed limit. It's a story crafted by fear and societal pressure that says: "Youth is the time to chase dreams." Or "if you haven't done it by now, you never will. "But history, science, and life itself proves otherwise. Think about, how many people find their greatest passions and successes well into their 40s, 50s, 60s, and beyond. Also consider how much depth, wisdom, and life experience adds in a way that youth often cannot. Do you want to know the truth? Dreams belong to the dreamer—not a timeline. To start reframing my fear of starting "late", I had to ask myself yet another question: "Why is it too *late*?" These fears are very real, but I wanted to be another example that they can be overcome.

Think about the most common regrets people have when

they face the end of life—they aren't usually about what they tried and failed at. They're about what they never tried at all. About the dreams they shelved, the risk they didn't take. Chasing a dream later in life doesn't mean you have to leap headfirst into the deep end. Sometimes the most sustainable way forward is through small, intentional steps. Each small step builds momentum. It chips away at the "too late" lie and fills you with evidence that you are capable.

Embrace a new definition of success. Success doesn't have to look like what you once imagined it would. Life changes, and so do dreams. My dream isn't about becoming famous or wealthy anymore. It's about creating meaning, connection, and joy. It's about healing myself and inspiring others to do the same. The intention behind my dream matters more than the scale of its achievement. By embracing my dream on my own terms, I was able to free myself from unrealistic expectations and open myself up to the richness of the journey itself.

I am the author of my story, pun intended, no matter my age or my circumstances, my story is still being written, I hold the pen; I decide what comes next. It's never too late to rewrite my narrative. To add new chapters filled with hope, courage and growth. Sure, at times I might look back on my life and I see the detours and delays, but these don't disqualify me from fulfilling my dream of becoming a Licensed Mental Health Counselor. Those detours and delays have prepared me. The wisdom, resilience, and strength I've gained are part of my unique advantage.

We were made for more than simply existing. We were made to dream, to create, to evolve—and to do so on your own timetable. So, if your heart is still whispering those dreams, listen closely. If you are still feeling that flicker of hope or passion, tend to it like a flame. Because it's never too late—not really. The only time it becomes too late to pursue a dream is when you stop believing it's possible. There was a time I thought the window had closed. That life had moved on without me, and the dream I once held so closely—to become a Licensed Mental Health Counselor—was no longer mine to chase. But something in me never stopped whispering. A quiet, steady voice that said, "You were made for this."

For years, I carried that dream silently. I've always had a heart for people—for the complexity of their stories, the resilience in their pain, the way love and trauma shaped how they show up in the world. I've always been the one others would confide in, the safe space, the listener. Deep down, I knew I wasn't just meant to give advice or offer comfort—I was meant to help others heal. And now… I am doing it. I'm going back to school. Not because it's convenient. Not because the timing is perfect. But because the dream never left—and I finally stopped ignoring it.

Going back to school isn't just about textbooks and late nights. It's about choosing *me*. It's about honoring my purpose after years of putting it off for other responsibilities, other people, or simply fear. It's about reclaiming something that always belonged to me: the belief that it's not too late to become who I'm meant to be. This journey is personal. It's scared. It's the beginning of a new chapter not just in my career, but in my healing, my growth, and my ability to help others navigate theirs.

It's not easy. There are days when doubt creeps in. Days when I wonder if I'll be able to juggle it all—work, family, finances, late nights of studying, early mornings of commitment. But then I remember: I'm not doing this just for a degree. I'm doing this because I want to help others heal their relationships, their families, and their inner worlds. I want to sit with people in the depths of their struggles and help them fine clarity, connection, and hope. Becoming a

Licensed Mental Health Counselor (LMHC) isn't just a career move—it's a calling. And answering that call means stepping into the unknown with both fear and faith, it means believing that every class, every paper, every challenge is bringing me closer to the life I was created to live.

As I pursue this dream, I'm not just studying theories and methods—I am becoming. I am becoming someone who believes in second chances. Someone who understands that healing is possible, no matter how long it's been delayed. Someone who refuses to live a life of "what ifs." I'm certain that this path will be hard at times, but I will not give up. Because this matters. People matter. I matter. And the version of me who once buried this dream out of fear finally gets to exhale—and rise.

The moment I choose to chase my dream—my age didn't matter—it was a gift. A gift from God who placed this my purpose on my heart, a gift to myself, to those who witnessed my bravery, and to the world that will benefit from me letting go of the fear and doubt to chase my dream. My dream matters because I matter, my story is unfinished, and the next chapter might be the most beautiful one yet. I see a future where I sit across from, couples, families, and individuals who feel broken, confused, or stuck—and I get to help them find their way back to each other and themselves. I see a future where my life experience, my compassion, my education, and my intuition all come together to create a space for healing and hope. And I'll remember that this future didn't arrive by chance. It came because I made a brave choice—to believe in my dream again. To bet on myself, no matter how long it's been.

Remember:

It's never too late to start.

It's never too late to believe.

It's never too late to dream—because your dreams are as timeless as your soul.

So, take a breath. Take a step. And stay true to yourself:

"I may not be where I once hoped to be, but I am here. And here is where I begin."

Because the truth is,

Dreams don't die. They wait. And you and I have waited long enough.

References

Pages 121-122; http://www.verawholehealth.com/careers/posts/self-awareness-recognizing-your-strengths-and-weaknesses

Page 127; https://humaans.io/hr-glossary/constructive-criticism

Page 146; https://medium.com/@EvolveMindset/the-importance-of-emotional-maturity-in-the-modern-world-d87c6d4fe872

Page 16; https://www.pinterest.com/pin/bakgrunner--759560293420942406/ "Pain grows when you don't grow from the pain." -C.C. Aurel

Page 55; https://www.biblestudytools.com/jeremiah/29-11.html#google_vignette "For I know the plans I have for you, plans to prosper you and not to harm you, plans to give you hope and a future." - Jeremiah 29:11

Page 85; https://www.pinterest.com/pin/50384089572075236/ "Life is not about expecting, hoping, and wishing; it's about doing, being, and becoming." -Mike Dooley

Page 115; https://genratec.com/eecummings/ "To be nobody but yourself in a world that's doing its best to make you somebody else, is to fight the hardest battle you are ever going to fight. Never stop fighting." – E.E. Cummings

Page 157; https://www.goodreads.com/quotes/12555391-one-day-you-will-tell-your-story-of-how-you "One day you will tell your story of how you overcame what you went through and it will be someone else's survival guide." – Brene Brown

NOTES:

Made in the USA
Middletown, DE
06 December 2025

24262408R00116